MOSAIC OF ORGANIZATIONAL

MOSAIC OF ORGANIZATIONAL CHANGE

GEORGE B. LAMPERE PH.D.

Published by Greer-Joel Publishing Company
1921 E. Tano Lane Mt. Prospect, Illinois 60056
www.greer-joel.com

Library of Congress Cataloging-in-Publication Data: 2015945436
Lampere, George B.
Mosaic of Organizational Change / George B. Lampere Ph.D. – 1st Edition.
p.   cm
00000000
ISBN-13 9780692252505 ISBN-10 0692252509 (soft cover)
1. Organizational Change-Management 2. Organizational Effectiveness
Printed in the United States of America

For my dad, in memoriam.

Acknowledgements

I OFTEN THINK OF my children, Ben and Jill and how much they have given me. They have developed into unique and interesting adults who have changed the way I look at myself and the world. Each has their own talents which they developed into a passion.

Jill is a professional esthetician and has a passion for making people look and feel good. She has beauty and uses her charm to guide me in being distinguished as I age. Jill will make sure that my eyebrows don't get too bushy. I resist when she tries to get me to put on a facial mask, but I know that her heart is in the right place to improve my looks. The photographs on the back cover my last book and this one were taken by Jill. She has taught me that feeling good about the way you look on the outside makes you feel good on the inside.

Ben (BJ), with his technical abilities has assisted me many times when I ran into problems writing this book, developing my web page, and all of the other computer-related glitches that I have encountered over the years. He has never complained and has jumped right-in giving me pointers and suggestions. I apologize for showing my frustration and calling you immediately when I impatiently encounter a problem. You have taught me to be more patient.

Jill and Ben became the people they are with the guidance and support of their mother, Jo-Ellen. She has raised them well and has been very patient with me for taking time to write this book. Jo-Ellen has taught me to be less stressed. I thank all of you for being there and for supporting me.

TABLE OF CONTENTS

Preface XIII

Chapter 1 Creating the Motion · 1

Chapter 2 Goal Setting: Top-Down and Bottom-up · · · · · · · · · · · · · · 6

Chapter 3 Lost Value – Lost Opportunity · 9

Chapter 4 Aligning Strategy with Execution - The Secrets to Success · · ·12

Chapter 5 Transformational Change Planning Essentials· · · · · · · · · · · ·16

Chapter 6 A Culture of Success and Sustainability· · · · · · · · · · · · · · · 20

Chapter 7 The Value of Dashboards ·23

Chapter 8 Business Policies that Shape Process · · · · · · · · · · · · · · · · 26

Chapter 9 Frustration with Software Applications · · · · · · · · · · · · · · · 30

Chapter 10 Independence and Transformational Change · · · · · · · · · · · 34

Chapter 11 Are You Abusing Your customers? · · · · · · · · · · · · · · · · · ·38

Chapter 12 A Three-Dimensional View of the World · · · · · · · · · · · · · ·41

Chapter 13 Creating a Workplace Culture with Mixed Generations · · · · 44

Chapter 14 Creating a Toxic Culture· 48

Chapter 15 Beyond Technology: Integrating Performance Drivers· · · · · ·51

Chapter 16 Information – The Lifeblood of Business· · · · · · · · · · · · · · 54

Chapter 17 The Three Levels of Need ·57

Chapter 18 When Technology is the Wrong Solution · · · · · · · · · · · · · 60

Chapter 19 Driving Value Though Business Processes· · · · · · · · · · · · · ·63

Chapter 20 Sustaining the Change · 66

Chapter 21 The Politics in Organizational Change · · · · · · · · · · · · · · ·69

Chapter 22 The Changing Role of Change Management · · · · · · · · · · · ·73

Chapter 23 Trust – Is Telecommuting Effective· · · · · · · · · · · · · · · · · ·76

Chapter 24 Adaptive Skills for Change ·79
Chapter 25 More than Business Intelligence ·83
Chapter 26 Influence and Persuasion· 86
Chapter 27 Communication for Learning ·89
Chapter 28 Employee Involvement and Commitment · · · · · · · · · · · · · ·92
Chapter 29 Using Rewards and Punishments for Change · · · · · · · · · · ·95
Chapter 30 Aligning Organizational Culture to Support Change · · · · · · ·98
Chapter 31 Collaborative Problem-Solving ·101
Chapter 32 Is Change Management worth it? · · · · · · · · · · · · · · · · · · ·104
Chapter 33 The Great Road Trip· ·107
Chapter 34 Guiding Principles for Transformation · · · · · · · · · · · · · · ·110
Chapter 35 Leadership in the Face of Change · · · · · · · · · · · · · · · · · · ·114
Chapter 36 Doing Bad Things Faster ·116
Chapter 37 Business Values of Peter Baily ·119
Chapter 38 Measuring Successful Change· ·122
Chapter 39 Making sacrifices to accomplish our goal?· · · · · · · · · · · · ·125
Chapter 40 Changing Minds and Behaviors ·128
Chapter 41 Pitfalls of Requirements Gathering · · · · · · · · · · · · · · · · · ·131
Chapter 42 What's Your Mobile Strategy? ·134
Chapter 43 Corps Leadership ·137
Chapter 44 Transformation – What does it really mean? · · · · · · · · · · ·141
Chapter 45 Rewarding Constructive Behavior· · · · · · · · · · · · · · · · · · ·144
Chapter 46 Clarifying Best Practices ·147
Chapter 47 Controlled Chaos · 151
Chapter 48 Eliminating Confusion about Process · · · · · · · · · · · · · · · ·154
Chapter 49 Managing Perceptions to Enable Change · · · · · · · · · · · · ·159
Chapter 50 Process Improvement Using Trial and Error · · · · · · · · · · ·162
Chapter 51 Lessons Learned from Major Change Initiatives · · · · · · · · ·167
Chapter 52 Communicating Change Effectively · · · · · · · · · · · · · · · · ·170
Chapter 53 Being Secure and Safe ·173
Chapter 54 The Rules that Killed a Business ·176
Chapter 55 The Right Personality for the Job · · · · · · · · · · · · · · · · · · ·180
Chapter 56 The Knowledge of Knowledge Management· · · · · · · · · · · ·184

Chapter 57 Effective Collaboration for Change · · · · · · · · · · · · · · · · · · ·188
Chapter 58 Business Continuity and large scale change · · · · · · · · · · · · · 191
Chapter 59 Lost in Translation ·194
Chapter 60 Resisting Change· ·197
Chapter 61 How Long Will It Really Take? · 200
Chapter 62 Does Your Job Fit You? ·203
Chapter 63 Not Your Typical Communication · · · · · · · · · · · · · · · · · · ·207
Chapter 64 Promoting Organizational Learning · · · · · · · · · · · · · · · · · ·211
Chapter 65 Team Size Matters· ·215
Chapter 66 The Goal of Organizational Change Management · · · · · · · ·219
Chapter 67 Behaviors that Fit the Job ·223
Chapter 68 The CEO's Role in Business Transformation· · · · · · · · · · · ·227
Chapter 69 Managing Trust ·231
Chapter 70 Making Change Communication Work · · · · · · · · · · · · · · ·235
Chapter 71 Structuring your Organization to Enhance Performance· · · ·239
Chapter 72 Fitting a Job like a Pair of Shoes · · · · · · · · · · · · · · · · · · ·243
Chapter 73 Using Lean Techniques in Service Industries· · · · · · · · · · · · 246
Chapter 74 Ten Key Ways to Adapt to Change · · · · · · · · · · · · · · · · · ·250
           About the Author ·255

PREFACE

THE LAST THING we need is another book on business transformation and organizational change management. How many ways can we manage our projects successfully, and how can I tell which methodology or approach is the best for my organization? Rest assured I did not write this book to tell you yet another way to manage change. I did, however, provide some things to consider as you enable change.

In discussions with my clients, I have shared stories and provided tips regarding various situations that exist within their project that have proved helpful. These tips and suggestions have proven themselves time and again to provide clarity and understanding in their change initiative.

Each topic is intentionally short, less than a thousand words to convey a message so you can get on with managing your project or apply these concepts in your daily business.

Some of the stories are analogies while others are just bits of information that may be useful in our change journey. To keep things interesting, each chapter starts with an interesting quote from a notable person. I found these quotes thought-provoking.

There is no real order or logic used to order these stories; it was just random thoughts that I just put together to share. It was my intent to keep the stories short and simple so you may be able to use the information on your next change initiative. I hope that you enjoy them.

1

CREATING THE MOTION

"We keep moving forward, opening new doors, and doing new things, because we're curious, and curiosity keeps leading us down new paths."

— WALT DISNEY

ORGANIZATIONAL CHANGE OCCURS each and every day. The business gets new customers and loses others. New products and services are introduced while others are phased out. Employees join the organization while others choose to leave; new governmental regulations dictate the way we must run our business, and new software applications with enhanced features and functionality are updated on a regular basis. Employees have learned to adapt to these changes in the course of their daily routine. In fact, organization change on average occurs at a rate of 2 percent per month according to researchers at Northern Illinois University. This means that a typical business will have to completely replace, delete, or update all of their records, software, and even training materials about every 3 to 4 years! You don't believe it?

Well, just look at how many times your cell phone or personal computer needs to be updated.

> "Managers seem to focus on the activity and not the outcome."

These changes have an impact on nearly every aspect of the business. The employee's need the ability to make informed decisions, quickly and effectively. The process must be designed in a way in which workflows through the organization and out to the customer, providing an expected level of quality and satisfaction. The technology that is selected and used should add value to the process by automating manual, administrative tasks, and integrate multiple systems to share data. Then there is the data itself. The right data is turned into useful information and shared with others to effectively problem-solve and make informed decisions.

When one area changes, it will have a direct impact on the other areas of the business, resulting in potentially negative consequences.

When an organization undertakes a large-scale project, managers seem to focus on the activity and not the outcome. The driver behind many of these initiatives is often the technology due to its level of complexity and associated cost. Software and other technology certainly can be shown to drive operational performance through its automation, integration, and collaborative capabilities. However, there are three other drivers of operational performance: business processes, people, and organizational systems; and information and knowledge management. Each one of these drivers can demonstrate measurable results by themselves. Combined, the whole is greater than the sum of each part. Each performance driver must not only be aligned, but also integrated so that the capabilities can be leveraged effectively and completely.

Consulting companies and program managers will often label their large-scale project as a "transformation initiative". Is this just "consultant ease" used to label any large project and command more money for consulting services, or does the word "transformation" actually imply a certain type of project? Can an organization actually have a large-scale project without labeling it a transformation initiative? It also can be referred to as a business transformation. A transformative initiative means to change radically from the current state to a defined future state.

When one of these performance drivers is changed without addressing the others, then the change will adversely impact the other areas. Implementing the automated features and functionality offered in the new software, will change the business processes and alter the job role by eliminating tasks that were once performed manually. The information will pass through the system faster and with a higher level of quality that will affect the amount of time that an employee needs to process their task, thereby changing their performance standards.

> "...every project is a change management project."

While the software architects, developers, testers, and other technical specialists focus on configuring the system, the people and organizational systems need to be managed by organizational change management (OCM) specialists. Many people are under the perception that the role of change management is to communicate the change to employees and then train them to use the new application. Communication and training are activities that are part of a total solution. There are many other activities that need to be planned and executed to achieve the desired results. These tracks of work include: Change Vision Alignment; Program Branding and Behavioral Based Communication; Stakeholder Management; Organizational Culture and Alignment; a Target Operating Model; Organizational Learning and Knowledge Management; and Transition Planning. Although many business and project managers believe that change management is needed, the truth is that every project is a change management project.

Organizational change management is a framework for managing the effects of new business processes, technologies, knowledge management and alignment of the organizational structure and cultural changes within an enterprise to achieve lasting success. Simply put, OCM addresses the people side of change. Organizational change management applies a structured process and set of tools for leading the people side of change to achieve the desired outcome.

There are two primary objectives of organizational change management:

75. Create awareness and understanding of the change vision by creating a sense of urgency and excitement to **support** the defined transformational initiative.
76. Identify and develop the new behaviors that are needed to **sustain** the change vision and remove barriers that prevent the organization from achieving its goal.

"The best-laid plans of mice and men often go awry." This quote from the book, Of Mice and Men written by the Nobel Prize-winning author John Steinbeck published in 1937 summarizes the plans of a typical transformation initiative. No matter how good the plan, there is always something that is unexpected that appears that will derail the plan. Even if everything goes perfect, there are still adjustments, tweaks, and corrections that need to be made. Don't forget, with the change occurring at a rate of two percent per month, how much change occurred after the plans were made and approved? A good rule of thumb to use for planning purposes is the 80 / 20 rule. If everything goes right, in the end, your project will reach 80 percent of the defined goal. Therefore, include extra resources at the end of the project devoted to performance improvements.

When we use the 80/20 rule to measure the goal of the change initiative, replacing only the technology and ignoring the business process, knowledge management, and people will only achieve 20 percent of the desired goal.

When a transformation initiative is chartered, one of the first activities is to define the business problem that the project will solve, and clearly define the vision of the change. Too often, projects are formed to replace a software application that is no longer supported, integrate systems after a merger, or consolidate financials for reporting. These may or may not be classified as transformation initiatives. However, the opportunity exists when efficiencies can be gained from people, process, technology, and information. The only way to determine if there is a gain in efficiency is to define and implement metrics and measures before, during and after the project.

All activities must have a well-defined outcome that is measurable against the goal and vision of the project. Too many projects focus on deliverables and tasks. If the task and deliverable do not add value, then it is not worth doing.

2

Goal Setting: Top-Down and Bottom-up

"When it is obvious that the goals cannot be reached, don't adjust the goals, adjust the action steps."

— Confucius

GOAL SETTING IS an important activity for every employee within the organization, but often many organizations do not incorporate this as part of their business practice, mainly because they do not understand the value to the business. Some organizations use goal setting as part of an employee's personal development plan where individual performance can be evaluated. Although individual goal-setting can be helpful to the employee, rarely it does not result in any noticeable change in the operational performance of the organization. Individual goal setting has in many cases been used to identify and improve a specific skill that is perceived to be below acceptable standards, i.e., to process a claim form within two hours with no mistakes. The improved efficiency and accuracy of the individual only serves to maintain a defined performance level and does nothing to raise the bar for the organization.

I was called to consult with a group of senior executives who were leading a process improvement initiative. They had hired a Tier 1 consulting firm who performed a high-level assessment in the procurement, human resources, and financial services functions of their hospital. In their final report, it identified an initial $10 Million dollars in cost savings by making some quick fix improvements that they called "low hanging fruit."

The senior executives told their department heads that the goal was to reduce the operating expense by $10 million dollars within the first year. This message was communicated to all of the employees throughout the hospital. The first reaction among the department heads was the anticipation of a budget cut. Employees, when questioned about the cost-cutting measures could not comprehend what they would do differently to reduce costs. The problem is how to translate the goal of $10 million dollar cost savings to the individual employee so they can understand and provide support and realize this higher goal.

The first step was to define an approach that would translate the goal from the conceptual level down to where individual employees could understand how their actions could reduce costs in measurable terms. A strategic plan was developed collaboratively by the senior leadership team to ensure that they understood and agreed to the overall approach.

It is important that every leader has a clear understanding of the goals and expectations of this initiative. This may require a group discussion to differentiate between a budget cut and ways to effectively eliminate non-value added activities. Not everyone may totally agree, but the leadership team must walk away with a clear vision of the initiative and understanding of acceptable and unacceptable cost reductions.

The next step is to define the current state business processes. The previous consulting firm narrowed the cost savings to three specific areas. It is now the responsibility of the project team to determine where potential disconnects, workaround activities, excessive wait times, or multiple handoffs are currently performed. It is helpful to create a process map and solicit the opinion of those employees who work within that process. Using a visual representation of how work flows through the process aids in clarifying real or potential issues. Then, determine the metrics and measures that are needed within the process from start to finish.

The third step is to determine the job role or position requirements within that process. This could include but not limited to: the various applications and other technologies used; the timing requirements to perform the task; the volume of tasks over a specific time; key decisions that need to be made, the information needed; the level of quality; and so forth. Then, determine the metrics and measures that are needed to perform the activities.

The fourth step in this goal setting process is to determine the competency fit of the individual employee to the job role or position within the business process. You will need to evaluate the knowledge, skills, ability, and behaviors of the employee and compare them to a defined position. Then determine the gap in each of the defined areas. This gap will define the need to support the individual goal.

The final step is to establish a goal that will support and align with the organizational goal. The supervisor and the employee should work together to define the individual's goal, the requirements, and the time requirements that are needed for success. The goals should be fairly challenging; where both parties are committed to supporting the goal. Finally, after concluding the negotiations, the employee should accept the goal.

When the individual goal is placed within the context of the overall organizational goal then, the employee can see the value. The organization will be able to realize their goal by cascading the requirements down to individual employees. It is at this point where employees can realize that their role is significant, and their actions or inactions can directly impact the overall performance of their organization.

3

Lost Value – Lost Opportunity

"The pessimist sees the difficulty in every opportunity; an optimist sees the opportunity in every difficulty."

— Winston Churchill

MANY ORGANIZATIONS TURN towards technology to improve their operational performance. The enterprise software application offers a wide range of features and benefits designed to automate tasks. These functions populate data from other sources, perform auto calculations and trigger workflow events. These features allow employees to collaborate by making it easier to send messages to other employees or to notify others that a task is complete. These feature rich enhancements are designed to save time and improve the quality of the information resulting in a perceived value to the business operation. However, often that value gets lost.

The enterprise software applications are designed to enhance business processes through integration of other software application functionality, standardize procedures across the organization using built-in business rules, automation of tasks, and collaboration using workflow. Problems occur when the enterprise software applications are used when business processes are not well defined, or not optimized to provide the most efficient operation.

Excel Corporation is a fictitious mid-market supply and Distribution Company in the mid-West. Excel employs approximately 460 people. The company has been experiencing slow but steady growth over the past couple of years and is planning on acquiring a small competitor who specializes in a unique product line. This acquisition will expand Excel's workforce by an additional 175 people.

Jill Smith is Excel's payroll manager. She has been working in this role for several years and has established a routine. Jill remembered writing payroll checks by hand and had transitioned to a desktop application about six years ago. Jill is the only person in the company that processes payroll and has been quite busy in her work. Now, with the addition of these new employees, she knows that it will be impossible to manage her workload and process the paychecks on time. Concerned about the increased workload, she discussed the situation with the Chief Financial Officer to hire a payroll assistant. The CFO stated that due to the acquisition, Excel is planning to purchase an Enterprise Resource Planning (ERP) software to improve the back office operations and reporting requirements. With the expansion and the plans to made significant capital purchases, the CFO rejected Jill's request. He suggested that she document her current process in preparation for the new ERP software and identify where any problems existed.

Frustrated, Jill returns to her office. She knows her payroll process and doesn't feel that she needs to write it down. She knows that the problem is just volume and doesn't believe that the new software will make much of a difference.

Within a few months, a consulting company was chosen along with the selection of a new enterprise system. The initial implementation focused on finance, human resources, and procurement. Payroll processing was part of the solution making it easier to track vacation accruals and post payroll to the general ledger. The consulting team gathered the requirements from Jill and configured the application. The consultants introduced new features and told her about some new functionality. She was too busy with processing the additional payroll that she did not have time to listen. She knew what she wanted and was comfortable doing the work as she knew how. Jill was unable to see the larger picture of how the integration and automation capabilities would save time.

Nearly ten months later the project was complete. The new ERP application integrated personnel and benefit records with payroll to improve the management of salary and wage records and well as tracking garnishments. A new web portal tool allowed employees to view their paycheck information.

Although these enhancements saved time, Jill spent more of her time tracking downtime reporting errors, running more payroll batches, and checking reports. She still felt overworked. Although the new software application greatly enhanced the transactional payroll processing, nothing was done to improve the business process or to fully leverage the application's capabilities allowing Jill to move away from heads down, low value administrative work, to a higher value, problem-solving and decision-making role.

The project was considered to be a success by Excel's executives by meeting the time, cost, and quality requirements. However, the organization lost the added value of time savings that the technology offered by not improving the business process, and lost an opportunity to leverage Jill's experience by changing her role to a knowledge worker.

A few months after the new application was implemented, Jill resigned her position and found a new company with hopes of less work stress and a lighter workload.

4

ALIGNING STRATEGY WITH EXECUTION - THE SECRETS TO SUCCESS

"However beautiful the strategy, you should occasionally look at the results."

— WINSTON CHURCHILL

STRATEGY AND GOALS set direction, but the execution drives results. How can senior leaders unify these often disparate paths to achieve their desired results? Setting strategic objectives, putting processes in place to achieve them, and realizing the results may appear to be simple—at least, in theory. In reality, organizations of all sizes struggle with making this happen. There are many symptoms, but at the heart of the problem lies three distinct silos within your business operation: strategy, analysis and execution and the gaps that exist across these critical functions.

Gap #1: The strategy silo. The strategy is set by the senior leadership in most organizations. The strategy is the set of ideas that align with the organization's mission and core values to achieve the desired goals. The strategy incorporates the organization's critical assets such as people (employees), technical and operational systems, information and knowledge, customers and suppliers. Understanding these resources and leveraging them to in certain ways to define calculated objectives is a strategy.

The strategy silo should ideally align and collaborate with the analysis and execution silos, but most often it does not. However, before you can effectively tackle that challenge, it is important to standardize your strategy efforts as much as possible. Otherwise, you end up with mini-silos within your strategic planning efforts, and this just adds to the chaos and further hinders results.

Tip #1: Use a standardized model for strategy planning. Decisions generate action that produces definable outcomes. Organizational outcomes are the consequences of the decisions made by its leaders. The framework that guides and focuses these decisions is a strategy. A strategy model aids in combining the strengths and weaknesses, opportunities and threats into a big-picture view that allows others to have a clear understanding and specific definable objectives. However, an understanding without the means to analyze and optimize your use of assets in an effective way—i.e. through effective processes—leaves you with nothing but a bunch of pictures and strategic plans that collect dust on your bookshelves.

Gap #2: The analysis & optimization silo. An analysis & optimization silo often results from attempts to improve the organization's business operations often with a driving focus on improved technical capabilities.

Technology managers and specialists focus on configuring the networks, data, system capabilities, and functionality to support the immediate needs of the business. Some of these changes are considered by the IT specialist and will be transparent to the end users. Some of these changes will alter the way work is performed.

Some of the technical changes may be easily understood and learned by the end user. The business managers may not immediately realize how this enhancement will change work procedures, business processes, reporting relationships and job roles.

The optimization of operational performance, collaboration, and level of quality achieved by the technical changes is greatly decreased or lost if the business does not make the necessary changes.

Tip #2: Analyze the technical performance equally in relation to business processes, people/organization, and information/knowledge management. The technical systems alone drive about 25% of the total operational performance. The business processes, people and organizational systems, and the information and knowledge management capabilities also drive operational performance. These four groups of performance drivers have equal weight, each adding 25% to the desired goal. Using the synergistic effects of each performance driver will increase the desired capability tenfold. The whole is greater than the sum of its parts.

Gap #3: The execution silo. It is easy to focus on the functional details of a technical solution for the configuration of the software application, establishing new functional parameters, building interfaces to other related systems and document new procedures. The primary issue is that the gap becomes wider between the strategy silo, the analysis, and planning silo, and the execution silo. The question of "what is the business problem" is never addressed, and the solution is rarely validated against the configuration of the application. All too often, the application configuration is based partly upon the current functional business tasks while the other requirements are based on the new features and functionality of the new system. As these new capabilities are implemented, other aspects of the business can become strained resulting in a new set of issues.

Tip #3: Align the strategy with the execution. Each set of activities and tasks performed should not be done in a technical, process, knowledge, or people silo that is often the case, especially if the project is technical in nature. Each activity and task should be validated against the change vision. Does this task help solve the business problem? What is the outcome of this task? How will we measure the effectiveness of the task against the change vision and the other performance drivers?

The Secret to Success is to close the gaps. There are a series of activities that need to be performed in a logical, sequential order to move from the strategic plan to executing the solution. The activities are grouped into four drivers of performance: people and organizational systems; business processes; technical systems: and information and knowledge management. Too often senior leaders or program managers may make assumptions regarding the level of understanding of a task; take a short cut to save time and money to complete the program; or may not realize how the changes will impact the business operation.

There are four levels of activities within each performance driver. These are defined as Strategic level, tactical level, operational level, and the functional level.

- The strategic level activities ensure that the organization has the right philosophies, values, beliefs, and understanding to support and align the change across each performance driver. Once these tasks have been completed, they move to the next level.
- Tactical level activities examine the capabilities and plan to achieve the change vision. The tactical activities focus on gathering business and technical requirements, establish metrics for success and will examine the current capabilities needed for execution.
- Operational level activities focus their attention on how the business continues to operate at acceptable service levels while the change vision is being planned and executed.
- The functional level activities look at the individual activities and tasks that will need to change as a result of the new initiative.

Summing Up: Business leaders and employees will be able to translate the change vision into a meaningful and measured outcome. This is done by aligning and sequencing the activities and tasks across each performance driver and the transition from the strategic level to the functional level.

5

TRANSFORMATIONAL CHANGE PLANNING ESSENTIALS

"Transformation literally means going beyond your form."

— WAYNE DYER

TRANSFORMATIONAL CHANGE REQUIRES a well-defined and articulated plan. Therefore, how do we plan effectively, and what are the features of a good change plan? Proper planning is essential to the execution of any large-scale change. Planning must be an inherent and fundamental part of the leadership and control, and managers are the single most important factor in effective planning. Navigating large-scale and transformative change demands a flexible approach that adapts specific planning methods to each situation, taking into account the activity being planned.

Transformational change involves many aspects of the organization. This planning approach must encourage rather than stifle innovation and creativity; enhance the quality of problem-solving and decision-making; promote customer and employee satisfaction, and promote the superiority of product and service offerings.

Transformational change depends on insight and collaboration in the managers and key stakeholders who support them. Collaboration is an advanced highly disciplined process that has been tested and proven to deliver the desired results in a short timeframe. It offers sufficient flexibility to fit into the planning scenario: it results in more aligned and impactful business planning; it ensures a sharp focus on issues and opportunities leading to customer-centric solutions, and it produces a much higher return on investment for resources deployed toward the initiative. When considering the current business dynamics and level of complexity, the organization needs to prevail in today's environment. In the future, the organization has no choice but to adopt this process if it is to maintain or improve its competitive position in the marketplace.

Planners must be always sensitive to the importance of tactical and operational cadence and ensure the planning facilitates rather than being inhibited. In fact, effective planning should accelerate the cadence by anticipating decisions and actions. The emphasis is on ensuring the progression while the guiding principles should not be viewed as an unbending rule. Leaders should weigh the advantages of acting more quickly against the advantages of preparing more thoroughly.

Transformational change requires plans with the proper level of detail, neither so detailed that they squash the initiative nor so general that they provide insufficient direction. The proper level of detail depends on each situation and is no easy task to determine. As a rule, plans should contain only as much detail as required to provide subordinates the necessary guidance while allowing as much freedom of action as possible.

Effective transformational planning is based on the recognition that change is intrinsically uncertain and unpredictable. Effective planning seeks not to eliminate uncertainty and risk, but to provide a framework that facilitates effective and focused action in the face of uncertainty and risk. Effective planning also recognizes the limits of foresight in a complex and changeable environment in the industry, and the world. Effective planning does not try to impose precise order and control in the business – trying to turn the business into something it is not. Instead, planning should provide enough structure to facilitate necessary cooperation and direction, but not so much structure that we sacrifice flexibility, tempo, or initiative. Recognizing the proper balance in any given situation requires judgment.

An integrated planning approach sees planning not only as a way of directing and coordinating actions but also of generating shared situational awareness and expectations., It supports the exercise of initiative and structuring the thinking of senior leaders, stakeholders, and planners. An integrated planning approach emphasizes planning as a continuous learning and adapting process rather than as a scripting process. Transformational planning requires the ability to extemporize—to be able to depart from the original ideas and concepts to exploit innovative opportunities and to collaboratively plan provides the point of departure for such adaptation in execution.

An integrated approach to planning emphasizes the importance of establishing clear objectives even as it recognizes the difficulty of doing so in a complex, uncertain, and shifting environment. Effective planning should proceed from after establishing clearly defined and measurable goals and objectives. The planning activities should examine the capability of the organization to actually achieve the goals, based on the maturity level of current technologies, business processes, staffing levels, and the ability to process information into knowledge. These capabilities are determined during the planning process at the strategic level. Once an acceptable strategic plan is defined, it should be responsive to the detailed requirements at the tactical, operational, and functional levels for proper execution.

An integrated approach to planning is based on the belief that in a typically complex and shifting situation, the best approach is usually to plan a rough outline and delegate as many decisions as possible to subordinates empowered to act on their own authority. In order to act appropriately, these subordinates require a thorough understanding of the overall vision and goal, which can only be provided by senior leadership.

There is a quote from Sun Tzu in the book, The Art of War, which states, "Victorious warriors win first and then go to war, while defeated warriors go to war first and then seek to win." In order to win or, in other words, to be successful it requires a well thought-out and executed plan.

6

A CULTURE OF SUCCESS
AND SUSTAINABILITY

"Success means having the courage, the determination, and the will to become the person you believe you were meant to be."

— GEORGE SHEEHAN

HAVE YOU EVER wondered why some organizations are very successful and remain that way year after year while similar organizations seem to struggle, just to survive? Moreover, have you wondered why some organizations that were once successful seemed to fade away, and eventually die?

I strongly believe that the success of an organization and its ability to maintain their competitive advantage is directly related to its culture. Those behaviors can be directly measured against their outcomes in terms of innovation and adaptability; problem-solving and decision-making qualities; customer and employee satisfaction; and quality of service and products.

Every critical decision you make, the way that you behave, the actions of your co-workers, and even the expectations we have about how we interact within our organization is, in fact, how we define organizational culture.

Work climate is different from organizational culture in that the climate changes like the weather, one day we are all smiles and happy, and the next day doom and gloom depending upon the situation at the time. On the other hand, Organizational culture, is deeply engrained, starting with the core values defined and reinforced by the leadership. The way jobs are defined; the interaction with other employees and the reporting relationships are part of the cultural rules that determine what is and is not acceptable behavior. Those people who buck the system and resist conformity to the unwritten rules may be punished, become frustrated and may choose to leave. Others who comply with the behavioral norms will be accepted and may be promoted.

The organizational culture extends beyond people and is built into the technologies that we use. Software applications are designed be adapt to meet the various business needs. These requirements are defined by the same key stakeholders who shape the policies and enforce the rules as they see fit. The various screens and fields within that application are defined based on the expectations of how work is to be performed. Access to view, edit, or delete information has been programmed into the system thereby reinforcing those expected behaviors. The ability to make certain decisions is based as much on the culture as it is in the authority you have based on your role.

Organizations that have been successful over a period of time, generally have a culture that is adaptive to change, and provides constructive support and encouragement. They have learned to translate their core values into actionable activities that promote constructive behaviors that reinforce the principles they espouse. Constructive behaviors maintain a healthy balance between supporting their employees and completing tasks that provide value to their customers.

Over time, a culture may shift, setting aside those core values replacing it by the stress and demands of the business. This occurs when immediate internal needs take priority. As the organization grows and matures, it can become complex and difficult to maneuver. The bureaucracy often will create inefficiency and inflexibility. As a result, the ability to be innovative and adapt to change comes to a halt. Customers and employees will become frustrated as the level of quality diminishes. Left uncorrected, the company will fail to maintain its competitive advantage and will eventually fail.

Successful organizations measure the behavioral drivers that define their cultures, such as leadership styles, communication quality, use of rewards and punishments, job design, and reporting relationships. In addition, these organizations also measure their cultural outcomes as I identified previously: innovation and adaptability; problem-solving and decision-making qualities; customer and employee satisfaction; and quality of service and products. Cultural outcomes are the consequences of the behaviors that exist within the organization. Consequences may be negative or positive. Outcomes can greatly influence results. Measures such as profit and market share are results that do not always show a strong correlation to outcomes. However, many research studies have proven that organizations that support a strong adaptive and constructive culture show a financial ROI of 600:1. These drivers and outcomes are measured by defining them as key performance indicators (KPI) or service level agreements (SLA). Other measures could include the participation in a customer loyalty program, the number of "likes" on Facebook, or other means to capture customer satisfaction.

7

THE VALUE OF DASHBOARDS

"Where is the wisdom we have lost in knowledge? Where is the knowledge we have lost in information?"

— T.S. ELIOT

WHAT WE SEE has a profound effect on what we do, how we feel, and who we are. Through experience and experimentation, we continually increase our understanding of the visual world and how we are influenced by it. In today's fast-paced, highly complex business environment, dashboards are becoming essential tools for keeping a pulse on the key elements within the business.

The dashboard is often a collection of graphical information that is displayed on dials, charts, and gauges that interpret data in the form of numbers, into a graphical image. Research has shown that the human brain deciphers image elements simultaneously while numbers are decoded in a linear, sequential manner, taking more time to process. Our ability to quickly decipher information is valuable when quick decision-making is needed. However, the real value of the dashboard is when key performance indicators (KPI's) and service level agreements (SLA's) are used to define which data to use to define the dashboard. There are many things that can be measured, but only those elements that are critical to the operation of the business are important. Measuring both the KPI's and SLA's can provide the context we need to make the information on the dials and charts meaningful.

To further illustrate my point, let's use the dashboard on your car as our analogy. The car's dashboard most likely has a speedometer, a gas gauge, oil pressure, and the water temperature as the basic instrument cluster. There are also some additional indicator lights. If we are traveling at 50 miles per hour, that speed is meaningless unless we place it within the context of the posted speed limit. If the speed limit was posted at 35 miles per hour, then we need to react immediately to slow our speed down to avoid a ticket. In my car, the oil pressure and the temperature gauges do not indicate whether they are within normal operating range or not. For this reason, I have no idea if a problem exists or not. I can make an assumption that if the indicator is at the bottom or the top of the scale with either of those two gauges then there may be a problem, but I would be guessing.

We must not look at the indicators as individual gauges but analyze the instrument panel collectively to provide us with a deeper understanding of the overall performance of our car. If the speedometer is losing speed, and the oil pressure gauge is low, and the water temperature is high we can say that the car has developed a serious problem that requires quick attention. There are times when the check engine indicator light comes on without any other sign of engine trouble. We make assumptions that if we do not hear anything rattle or bang, see a puff of black smoke or lose power that everything must be ok. Can we assume that the sensor is bad or set wrong? Many times we do just that, ignore a potential problem. I had a friend that placed a piece of electrical tape over the check engine light because it remained lit. Then one morning when he was heading off to work, the car would not start. It turned out to be a problem with his catalytic converter that eventually blocked the exhaust system.

The information presented on a dashboard should be designed to measure critical elements within your business. Each gauge should indicate pre-defined control limits to determine if the information is trending up or down. Indicator lights and alarms should reflect realistic limits that would cause someone to react to the situation. The gauges should provide a context among the other indicator gauges to display the overall performance and health of the business operation. Most importantly, the dashboard is only as valuable as the person who interprets the information. Dashboards are a valuable and powerful tool in the hands of a skilled operator who has the knowledge, skills, and authority to problem-solve effectively and make quick, informed decisions.

8

BUSINESS POLICIES THAT SHAPE PROCESS

"Our differences are policies; our agreements, principles."

— WILLIAM MCKINLEY

I HAD THE OPPORTUNITY to provide some consulting work for a financial institution to help them improve their operational processes. The company was implementing a new enterprise software application, and the unit manager wanted this opportunity to enhance many of the key end-to-end processes that were impacted by the software.

Prior to my arrival, several groups within the project team were mapping these processes to a level of detail showing the activities and tasks within swim lanes that indicated those who were responsible for the tasks. I was impressed with the amount of work that was already accomplished. Each process map indicated key decision points and links to software applications that automated a task. The manager stated that the next big project task was to define the policies and procedures.

Concern was shown on my face with the manager's statement. Noticing the distress, he asked what was wrong. Holding the pile of process maps in my hand, I asked him how they were created without knowing the policies. He did not see the connection. There was an assumption that the policies and procedures were similar to the process narratives or descriptions. The education started at that point.

Before a business process can be developed, we must understand the business policies and rules that define the process. With these guidelines in place, the business process can be defined to a level of detail showing how activities and tasks are performed and controlled. The policies and rules will determine things such as the level of approval authority, go-no-go decisions, acceptable risk, service levels, and key performance requirements.

On the other hand, Procedures, are similar to work steps. These are the guiding instructions to perform a task. Procedures can only be developed after the process has been defined since the process identifies the workflow and the policies and rules that determine their governance.

Business policies are guideline statements that define the scope and area of influence and control that determine which decisions can be made by subordinates within the organization. It permits the lower-level management to deal with the problems and issues without consulting top-level management every time a decision is required. Some business policies are developed in response to a particular situation that may have had the potential to place the organization at risk. Other business policies are developed and implemented to standardize and control operational procedures to ensure consistency. However, policies that may have minimized the risk or established working standards may no longer be applicable. Over time, the factors that once influenced the situation may have changed, no longer creating a risk. The policy subsequently may become a limiting factor or even a barrier to sustaining operational performance.

A business rule is an operation statement that defines or constrains aspects of the business operation and almost always resolves to either a true or false decision. Business rules are used to influence and control the behaviors of the business. These rules can apply to people, processes or technology systems within the organization and are put in place to help the organization achieve its goals. An example of a business rule may state that contracts over two million dollars will require legal review or payment terms must be net thirty days. Business rules are often informal or even unwritten. The informality of these rules can create a great deal of confusion to misinterpreting the intent. Over time, these rules may evolve into a completely different meaning and be treated as a policy. To avoid such confusion, rules should be well-documented to ensure the purpose and intent are understood.

DESIRED OUTCOMES

All of the business policies and business rules within the scope of the change initiative need to be identified and evaluated to ensure that the business goals, mission, and vision can be achieved.

PLANNING CONSIDERATIONS

Identify the business policies and documented rules that are within the scope of the change initiative. An effective business policy or business rule must have the following features:

1. Specific: The policy or rule should be specific. If it is uncertain, then the implementation will become difficult.
2. Clear: The policy or rule must be unambiguous. It should avoid the use of jargons and connotations. There should be no misunderstandings in following the policy.
3. Reliable and consistent: The Policy must be uniform enough so that the subordinates can efficiently follow it.
4. Appropriate: The policy or rule should be appropriate to the present organizational goal.
5. Simple: The policy or rule should be simple and easily understood by all in the organization.

6. Inclusive and comprehensive: In order to have a wide scope, a policy or rule must be comprehensive.

7. Flexible: The policy or rule should be flexible in operation/ application. This does not imply that a policy or rule should always be altered, but it should be wide in scope so as to ensure that the line managers use them in repetitive/routine scenarios.

8. Stable: The policy or rule should be unwavering; else it will lead to indecisiveness and uncertainty in minds of those who look to it for guidance.

9

FRUSTRATION WITH SOFTWARE APPLICATIONS

*"I've come to believe that all my past failure and frustration
were actually laying the foundation for the understandings that
have created the new level of living I now enjoy."*

— TONY ROBBINS

WHY DO BUSINESSES have issues with their software applications? I had asked myself this question after talking with several frustrated managers about their systems. Nearly every manager blamed the software for, not functioning properly, and was ready to replace it. "It is a piece of garbage" one manager exclaimed, clearly agitated over their inability to perform routine business tasks like generating purchase orders or inventory control. Another manager stated that the software application had created more work than doing the same task manually.

It would have been easy to jump to conclusions why these managers had issues with their software, citing lack of training and operator error. However, these problems did not occur immediately after the software was installed, but rather the problems started to be reported a year or two after implementation. The complaint was not with one specific application or software publisher, but rather the complaints came from all over: large and small businesses and different industries.

When investigating deeper into the problem, I found that the issues varied greatly. Some of the problems indeed stem from a lack of training while other issues were caused by bad data, improper configuration, and network performance. I was determined to identify a common cause, or theme that would lead to stress and frustration.

I had to rule out the software application being the cause of the problem since it was not specific to one vendor or type. I had to look at other factors that related to the software application such as the environment, the time frame, and the implementation. After assessing many of these factors, I came up with some interesting findings.

Cultural Environment: Most employees report they are skilled in performing their tasks and know what is required to achieve an acceptable level of efficiency and quality. There is a sense of pride in their work and the need to be recognized by their managers and peers. As a result, these employees will make assumptions that can lead to incorrect actions. Employees may short cut steps in a procedure to improve efficiency, or even tell others they know how to use a particular application when they do not have the proper training or knowledge. These bad habits become an acceptable practice and get passed along to other employees that may have unforeseen negative consequences.

Time Frame: Implementing new software applications takes time for planning, development, implementation, testing, and training. Time away from the actual daily work activities is seen as costly and unproductive. For this reason, the quicker the application is installed, the sooner the business will be productive again, is the attitude of most managers. On the other hand, the business evolves: new client demands, shifting economic conditions, changes in suppliers, and government regulations will change the way business is conducted. Research shows that the average rate of change is two percent per month. For this reason, the business needs to accommodate for the change over time and adjust accordingly. The software application must be flexible and easy enough to make changes to accommodate the evolving business needs. Time is needed during the planning phase to not only address the current needs of the business, but also anticipates the near term, future needs as well. This will save time and energy in the long term.

Implementation: Most managers are not accustomed to working in a project environment or implementing software. They are not aware of the importance of each phase of the project and the amount of effort needed to integrate a system into an existing business. Their point of reference is implementing Microsoft Office on their desktop. The software guides them through each step to perform a standard implementation. Microsoft office has 150+ user defined settings. In a recent survey of Microsoft users, it indicates that less than 5% of the users had changed any settings at all. More than 95% had kept the settings in the exact configuration that the program installed. Therefore, the assumption is made that the business application works similarly. "Let's just install it now, and we can make changes later if needed", or "let's get the system in now and worry about the process changes later," are some of the comments that I hear on the project.

Implementing a software application requires much more than just the installation of the software and converting the data. The software application is a tool that enhances the business process to make it more efficient and enables the employees to shift from laborious administrative tasks to more customer-focused problem-solving and decision-making activities. The integration, automation, and workflow capabilities in the software will change the service-level agreements (time) and the key performance indicators (quality) at the functional level. For this reason, the business process along with the performance measures will have to change to accommodate for this new functionality. Failure to make adjustments to these areas will not only create inefficiencies but will promote problems to occur faster and more frequent.

These common factors: Cultural Environment, Time Frame, and Implementation all contributed to the current issues in the software and the attitudes about the application. These issues could be greatly reduced by creating a comprehensive implementation plan that includes:

- Following a well-structured project plan
- Allowing time for assessment of the current state
- Identification of future state needs
- Addressing people and organization system requirements
- Define and document business processes
- Leverage available technical capabilities
- Management of information to create workplace knowledge.

The time spent in planning for change will be less costly than battling changes and dealing with the frustration it created.

10

Independence and Transformational Change

"If we can recognize that change and uncertainty are basic principles, we can greet the future and the transformation we are undergoing with the understanding that we do not know enough to be pessimistic."

— Hazel Henderson

The Fourth of July is a holiday that most Americans celebrate for various reasons. The festivity may involve family, friends or public gatherings. Flags wave, bands march and bystanders cheer. The parades are pageants, visible spectacles for all to applaud and enjoy. After the confetti blows away, what is the meaning of the day? Allow me to reflect on the history before I make my point. The original thirteen colonies sought to become independent states, no longer under the rule of the British Crown. The goal of the rebellion was to gain self-government, for each colony and to establish a state sovereignty for each Commonwealth. In a famous letter written by John Adams on July 3, 1776, to his wife Abigail he stated, "… You will think me transported with Enthusiasm, but I am not. I am well aware of the Toil and Blood and Treasure that it will cost us to maintain this Declaration and support and defend these States. Through all the Gloom, I can see the Rays of ravishing Light and Glory. I can see that the End is more than worth all the Means…."

Many members of the Second Continental Congress voted to approve a resolution of independence proposed by Richard Henry Lee of Virginia. The members had a strong desire to change deeply founded by their common belief in a common set of values. When Thomas Jefferson drafted the formal declaration, he placed into writing the clear vision for change. Although the document reflected many of the shared beliefs of the colonies, not everyone embraced the idea. Of the 13 colonies, nine voted in favor of the Declaration, two -- Pennsylvania and South Carolina -- voted No, Delaware was undecided, and New York abstained. There were many people who wanted to remain under British rule, keeping things the same. They knew that the freedom would be costly, but despite the ongoing battle, the colonists were making progress. The Continental Army had forced the British to surrender at Yorktown, in 1779. The Americans has effectively won independence through the fighting would not formally end until 1783, a full seven years after the Declaration of Independence was signed.

What lessons can we take from this historic experience in transforming our business today? Allow me to compare the eight steps for successful change defined by John Kotter to the creation of the independence of the United States:

Establish a sense of urgency: Help others see the need for change, and they will be convinced of the importance of acting immediately. The colonists felt an urgent need to escape from the controls of the British and be free to live and govern as they saw fit.

Create a guiding coalition: Assemble a group with enough power to lead the change effort, and encourage the group to work as a team. It took the leadership of the Second Continental Congress to come together and develop a plan.

Develop a vision for change: Create a vision to help direct the change effort, and develop strategies for achieving that vision. Richard Henry Lee drafted a resolution calling for the political ties between Britain and the colonies to be dissolved. Thomas Jefferson drafted the Declaration of Independence which became the vision for change.

Communicate the vision for support and buy-in: Make sure as many as possible understand and accept the vision and a strategy. Although many colonists agreed in principle that the change was needed, they all did not agree to a written declaration at first; members needed reassurances and support.

Empower Broad-Based Action: Remove obstacles to change, change systems or structures that seriously undermine the vision and encourage risk-taking and nontraditional ideas, activities, and actions. The Continental Army was short on supplies during the Revolutionary war and called upon France to lend support to supply money, munitions, soldiers, and warships.

Generate Short term wins: The Plan for achievements that can easily be made visible, follow-through with those achievements and recognize and reward employees who were involved. There were a number of battles fought during the Revolutionary war, each providing short-term wins that eventually led to the British surrender.

Never let up: Use increased leadership to change systems, structures, and policies that don't fit the change vision. Hire, promote, and develop employees who can implement the vision, and finally reinvigorate the process with new projects, themes, and change agents. The Revolutionary war lasted nearly eight years. During that time, ambassadors from the colonies continued to build worldwide support from France, Spain, and the Dutch Republic.

Incorporate the changes into the Culture: Articulate the connections between the new behaviors and organizational success, and develop the means to ensure leadership development and succession. Following the Revolutionary War, the new United States adopted the Constitution on September 17, 1787, by the Constitutional Convention in Philadelphia, Pennsylvania. This was the supreme law that defined the behaviors of the new United States.

Every year since the signing of the Declaration of Independence, the United States celebrates with parades and fireworks. Organizations should also celebrate their transformation initiatives to create a sense of pride and unity. Transformational change is neither quick nor is it easy. With strong leadership that creates a clearly defined change vision that supports the core values of the organization, and guiding principles will result in measurable and lasting success.

11

ARE YOU ABUSING YOUR CUSTOMERS?

"Your most unhappy customers are your greatest source of learning."

— BILL GATES

D O COMPANIES INTENTIONALLY position their products or services to make their customers dependent upon them? In addition, is dependency a good or bad thing? Certainly from a marketing perspective, the desired consequence is to create a strong desire to use the product or service. The cell phone is a good example. Feature rich phones provide more than just phone calls. Texting, photographs, video, games, and even television shows can be accessed by this device. However, does it become abusive when the service provider of the cell phone limits or restricts certain applications? This was certainly the case brought against Microsoft in 2001 by the U.S. Department of Justice over the bundling of Internet Explorer. The Department of Justice alleged that Microsoft abused monopoly power on Intel-based personal computers in its handling of operating system sales and web browser sales. The issue central to the case was whether Microsoft was allowed to bundle Internet Explorer (IE) web browser software with its Microsoft Windows operating system. Bundling them together was alleged to have been responsible for Microsoft's victory in the browser wars as every Windows user had a copy of Internet Explorer. It was further alleged that this restricted the market for competing web browsers (such as Netscape Navigator or Opera) that were slow to download over a modem or had to be purchased at a store.

Can this same type of abuse occur at the operational level within a business? That question was raised by a group of mid-level executives and business consultants. That question required a great deal of defining and positioning. Their answers varied as much as the definition they used. The common definition used was as follows: In the day-to-day business operation between the company and the customer, can the product or service be positioned where the client is unknowingly placed in a position of dependency. The groups answer was in agreement. Without violating tort law, full disclosure is made to the client about features, functionality, terms and conditions with full consent without understanding their consequences. This occurs more often than not, creating a stressful situation between the customer and business.

The issue does not always stem from the way the contract was written, but rather the prevailing organizational culture. A strong, aggressive culture may push the sales representative to close the sale quickly. Due to the urgent need for the business to move forward, the word of the salesperson is taken over what was written in the fine print. Sometimes it is the reputation of the company that outweighs other considerations. A large, well-established company may create a higher level of trust and lower the risk of the product or service offering over an unknown.

A sale is not the only area where abusive practices can occur. Recently I signed up for a training class. I had the option of attending an instructor-led class or completing the course on-line. The facilitated course was considerably more money, so I chose the computer-based learning. That course consisted of a series of videos, a downloadable student guide, and a case study workbook. Within each lesson, there was either a step missing or an error in the instructions. Were these mistakes and oversights intentional to get me frustrated enough to take the most expensive classroom training, or was it a result of poor quality control? Whatever the intent, the operational culture was such that the behaviors of the employees did not value customer satisfaction or the quality of service and products? Satisfaction and quality are the outcomes of the culture that are measurable.

The attitudes and behaviors of the employees who produce inferior work are influenced by the organizational culture. Some may say it is a lack of supervision or controls. Increased supervision and quality controls will just put a spotlight on the issue and only temporarily solve the problem. Behaviors consistent over time among the employees may be indicative of the current culture. The lack of quality and poor performance at work may be due to one or several factors including leadership and managerial style, rewards and punishment, job design and reporting relationships, communication styles and more. Each factor contributes to the current behavior that in turn establishes expectations. Over time, employees become conditioned to the acceptable behavior that will turn into a prevailing culture. The factors along with the expectations will change from one department to the next. Department A may have a manager who is a strong leader and communicates well with his or her employees, but may not provide training and guidance on the job. Department B may enforce strict rules. Employees may not be rewarded for their efforts, but often will be punished for making mistakes.

The organizational culture is based upon the company's core values that are reinforced by the behavioral norms and expectations. To create a strong constructive and adaptive culture that aligns with the organization's core values, examine how employees interact with each other, the ability to work in empowered teams, the autonomy in their jobs, and their ability to contribute.

12

A Three-Dimensional
View of the World

*"The ultimate authority must always rest with the individual's
own reason and critical analysis."*

— Dalai Lama

THE WORLD IS not flat like a picture, but yet many people make critical decisions based on reports that are shown in two dimensions just like a picture. It appears that many business leaders rely on performance reports to give them a current view of their operation. Reports provide a single point of view. A person can only make assumptions as to what is happening outside of the framework of the picture. The report is a snapshot in time; a moment in history commonly represented by two dimensions such as transactions per hour. A bank statement, for example, is a report that shows all of the deposits and withdraws that occurred over the past month along with the ending balance. Although this is useful information to balance your checkbook, the information is old. The balance does not reflect the checks written since the statement, nor does it identify your reoccurring monthly expenses, major expenditures planned or anticipated revenue. For years, these two-dimensional reports were all that was available to business leaders to make decisions. Collecting, reporting and analyzing the data takes time and by the time the conclusion is reached, it may be too late. We need a better way to access, display and analyze information based upon multiple dimensions, moving from being reactionary to proactive planning and problem-solving.

The new business intelligence tools provide data from a business viewpoint. Online analytical processing or OLAP provides a multi-dimensional analytical query. OLAP consists of three basic analytical operations: consolidation (roll-up), drill-down, and slicing and dicing. OLAP is often referred to as a cube, referring to its three-dimensional nature. The technology now makes the analysis possible, however, many business leaders still think in terms of traditional two-dimensional reports. New decision-making behaviors will take the time to develop; these business leaders need to shift their paradigm. The process for making decisions changes from: "what information is needed to get an accurate view of the problem", to "what is the base course of action based upon the information".

Think of OLAP in terms of a Rubik's cube. In a traditional 2-D report, we see only the front of the cube, we can only assume how the top, right and left sides, back and bottom of the cube will look. Each side of the cube represents a different view that has a relationship, such as financial, sales, product, vendor, region, and market. Each cube can be represented by a project or

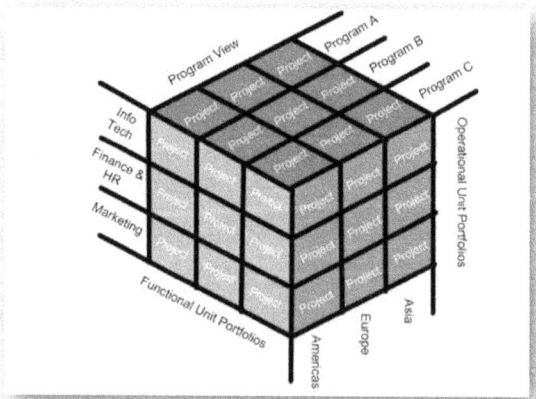

another initiative. With each parameter defined, we can now examine the cause-and-effect relationships, drill-down to specific cubes to examine the details, and inspect the impact that one parameter has on an individual or whole.

To further illustrate the power of the cube analysis let me describe a scenario. Our organization has three major programs currently underway. Each program consists of multiple projects. These programs span across three business units. There are three functional areas impacted by the three programs. We not only need to assess the overall impact the programs have on the organization, but also need to examine the individual projects.

In the diagram above, we can see the various dimensions: Program view, the Organization Business Unit view, and the functional unit view. With the information displayed in this fashion, it is much easier to answer the following questions:

- Who within the organization is being impacted the most by the change?
- What type of change are they experiencing?
- What degree of change are these business units and functional areas experiencing?
- Where is the greatest benefit felt?
- When will the change take effect?
- Why are some projects over budget?
- How the will a change in one business unit impact the other?

All of the information to our questions is contained within this cube in real time. Specific information that is relative to various leaders can be displayed on the dashboard of indicators that show upper and lower control limits. When the indicators exceed the limits, the business leader can drill down and around to identify the problem area easily.

13

Creating a Workplace Culture with Mixed Generations

"The primary reason we do too much is that we have never taken the time to discover that portion of what we do that makes the biggest difference."

— Peter Drucker

There's no arguing that the workplace is an ever-changing environment. As societal norms change, so does the culture of our organizations. As younger generations join the workforce, the dynamics change as their values and opinions impact the way organizations function and interact. At this point in time, there are three generations that are currently active in our workforce, and there's little doubt that having that wide of an age range in any organization is bound to come with challenges. In a recent study of generations in the workforce, this is what they found:

- 68% of Baby Boomers feel that "younger people" have poor work ethics, which in turn makes their work even harder.
- 32% of Gen X-ers also feel that the "younger generation" has a poor work ethic.
- Gen Y-ers, which have been called "the most high-maintenance, yet potentially most high-performing generation," believe they have a good work ethic for which they are not given enough credit.
- 13% of Gen Y-ers believe the difference in work ethics between generations cause friction in the workplace.

In addition, what is one of the biggest differences between these generations that are a constant cause of workplace tension? Technology! While Baby Boomers and Generation X-ers prefer phone communication and face-to-face business transactions, Generation Y-ers prefer to communicate via blogs, IMs, text messages, and emails. Generation Y sees this type of communication as effective and efficient while the older generation sees this as lazy and potentially harmful to business.

The Baby Boomers are the children of the Traditionalists, having been born during the "baby boom" that came after World War Two ended. This generation is comprised of those born from the years 1946 to 1964. The Baby Boomers are a very competitive generation, likely as a result of the huge population swell that occurred as a large number of children were born in this post-war era. Since so many people were coming of age all at once, there was intense competition for good jobs. As a result, the Baby Boomers typically feel that younger, less-experienced workers should have to pay their dues before they get a good job with a fancy title and an office. Baby Boomers have traditionally been motivated by competitive salaries and opportunities for promotions or career growth. This generational group is now reaching retirement age and being replaced by those who have greater technical experience and lower salaries.

Those born from 1965 to 1980 are commonly known as Generation X. Those from this generation were typically latch-key kids, born into families with two working parents, or perhaps divorced parents. As a result, this generation is typically very independent. Along with this independence comes skepticism – of everything from organizations to questioning other people's intentions. Gen Xers often like to work independently and don't enjoy micro-management. This group strives to find a work/life balance, unlike their overly competitive parents from the Baby Boomer generation. Those from this generation are typically entrepreneurial and have adapted well to technology as it has changed and evolved. They seek fun and meaningful work. They value the freedom to set their hours. Flexible work schedules and work-from-home options (as long as billable quotas are met), may help to retain and motivate this generation. A hands-off attitude often works best when supervising, mentoring or working with this generation. Coach, don't lecture them. Gen X-ers value freedom and autonomy to achieve desired goals and often prefer to work alone rather than in teams. They dislike "meetings about meetings" and don't want or need face time. Don't expect blind loyalty. Gen X-ers are supreme skeptics and cynics and value authenticity. They expect change. Gen X-ers thrive on diversity, challenge, responsibility and creative input. If their current firm does not provide them with these opportunities, they will not think twice to move elsewhere.

Those young up-and-comers who were born from 1981 to 1994 are known as Generation Y. This group comes from an era of technology – right from the time of birth. They are completely comfortable with technology because it is been woven into their lives from the very beginning. This group is also known for their tolerance of others, stemming from their comfort level with merged families and diversity. Generation Y is a highly sociable group that uses social media, cell phones, and the Internet to keep in touch with their friends, families and colleagues. Because of their social nature, this generation typically enjoys teamwork and wants to feel like a valued member of the organization. This group also enjoys frequent feedback on performance and can be very loyal to the organization.

Generation Y's need detailed instruction about what you want – but let them determine how to get there. Make the work relevant to them and important to them and the company. If you engage them, they will work hard. They are accustomed to new ideas and situations, a constant opportunity to learn (or more accurately find out).

Generation Y employees will be loyal to the company – but will not provide blind loyalty. As long as their personal interest and career needs are being met (which frequently change) – and the company is socially responsible, the Millennial will be loyal. However, they are not concerned about job-hopping. They will quit now and find that job later - and if that does not work out, they can always count on their helicopter parents for support. Praise them often daily and coach them.

Generation Z's were born from the mid-1990's to present. This group is the latest to join the workplace. This group tends to be very independent. They grew up in a healthier economy and are eager to learn from their own mistakes or others. Curious and driven, this group investigates how to obtain relevant professional experience before college. Despite their obvious technology proficiency, Gen Zers seem to prefer in-person to online interaction and are being schooled in emotional intelligence from a young age. Thanks to social media, they are accustomed to engaging with friends all over the world, so they are well prepared for a global business environment.

As with many issues of workplace diversity, it is important that all the members of your organization learn to work together harmoniously, creating an environment of mutual respect. This can be done by allowing your employees to build functional workplace relationships, creating a sense of understanding and acceptance of generational differences.

14

CREATING A TOXIC CULTURE

"Without exception, the dominance and coherence of a constructive culture proved to be an essential quality of the excellent companies."

— TOM PETERS

RECENTLY I WAS contacted by the CFO of a mid-sized company to provide suggestions to solve their financial reporting problems. Their company has been growing at a rapid pace since its founding ten years ago. The company now has satellite offices in eight locations throughout the United States and Canada. In addition to the offices, the company has a close affiliation with two manufacturing companies that produce their products.

The production, marketing, sales, warehousing, and financial leaders had been laser focused on keeping pace with their respective departments. The growth of the company quickly stretched the limits if the software systems. With each leader focused on their individual areas, application integration was not anticipated to be an issue. Now, it started to become evident to each department head that information sharing is needed to improve coordination of work throughout the organization to deliver the product to the customer on time and within defined requirements.

Over the past ten years, a culture was formed that promoted an aggressive culture that fostered specific behaviors among the employees. These included: Using the authority of their position to get things done; build up their power base; personally run everything; act forceful and maintain unquestioned authority. Each department was operating independently and, as a result, lost sight of the overall goal – to achieve the mission of the organization. They failed to operate as a well-coordinated and adaptable organization. This was a very toxic culture and the behaviors needed to change to save the company. Continuing down this toxic path would certainly divide the employees, creating mistrust and avoidance.

Organizations that are successful over a long period of time have an adaptive – constructive culture. Employees work to achieve self-set goals, pursue a standard of excellence, think ahead and plan, and take moderate risks. At the same time they show concern for others, they involve others in decision-making, resolve conflicts constructively, and help others to grow and develop. By creating these behaviors, my client would have anticipated the need for collaboration and information sharing between departments. The outcome of these behaviors leads to increased innovation and adaptability; improved problem-solving and decision-making; customer and employee satisfaction; and quality of products and services.

My first challenge was to help the leadership team create a long-term vision for change. This was not going to be easy since they were way too busy putting out fires and focused on their departmental issues. I needed the leaders to see how each department was pulling the organization in different directions, and that would severely hurt the organization. To achieve this vision for change, I talked to the company president who described the pain points and articulated her goals and expectations. Using that information, I spent some time interviewing key people and gathering information associated with the goal. Once I compiled this information, I brought all of the key leaders together for three facilitated work sessions over a six-week period. My goal was to create a long-term plan based upon a collaborative approach that would get the leaders aligned with the president's goals and expectations.

My Integrated Performance Solution provides a three-phase planning process that would guide leaders through a diagnosis of their business, to identify and evaluate value creating opportunities; develop a transformation strategy that would create an "Ideal" future state and a roadmap for change; then create a blueprint to focus the organization's energies on creating the future state. This structured approach creates buy-in and support through ownership in the formation of the plan. Using a top-down tactic, the leaders help remove obstacles, such as using disparate software applications, and just focusing on their department rather than the company. With a concerted effort to achieve the president's goal, the behaviors that once created, a toxic culture will slowly shift to a culture that is adaptable and constructive supported by the leadership. Now a planning process that was nearly nonexistent was formalized within six weeks. The initial problem of software integration was much deeper, but now can be addressed with clarity and purpose.

15

Beyond Technology: Integrating Performance Drivers

*"In business, words are words; explanations are explanations,
promises are promises, but only performance is reality."*

— Harold Geneen

THE PROCUREMENT PROCESS at an office supply store was not very effective and was in dire need of improvement. The store manager stated that some products were out of stock due to late or neglected order placements. Other products were overstocked, costing the organization thousands of dollars in inventory and taking up valuable warehouse space. Physical inventory did not match the amount indicated in their system. As a result, customers became frustrated and left the store without making a purchase and employees had become stressed over the abuse received by their customers, and the amount of time it took doing physical inventory counts.

Seeking outside assistance, the store manager turned to a consulting company to find an economical solution to their inventory management process. After listening to the manager's story, the consultant offered up a solution: a software application that integrates with the stores financial system to track inventory, vendors, and payments. The system was connected to their point-of-sale system to trigger a pre-set reorder point for inventory to ensure the projects arrived in time.

The new software system was implemented, and all of the employees received training. The automated features improved quality by the eliminating the mistakes made through manual entry of product counts, item numbers, and other data. The automated workflow promised to save both time and money through its efficiencies. The product did function as anticipated, but the store manager was not totally satisfied. She made the assumption that the employees would now have more time to perform other needed tasks around the store and possibly reduce the number of employees per shift, but that was not the case.

The store owner failed to look at all of the areas that drive operational performance. Attention was placed on the technology to integrate and automate many of the activities but failed to examine the changes in the business processes, the people and organization, and the information and knowledge management activities.

Business Process: The end-to-end flow of work from the supplier to customer needs to be efficient. Although the technology can enhance the process by improving the quality, and speed, it does not compensate for a faulty process. Technology, by its nature, will change Service level Agreements (SLA's), the time required to complete an activity and Key Performance Indicators (KPI's) the level of quality required for a particular activity. It will not improve the number of hand-offs needed to make a decision, or the time it takes to make a decision. An over-complicated or non-value added process will still decrease the overall performance.

People and Organization: The new software requires learning new competencies with a learning curve that could extend for six months. The job itself must change. Some of the tasks that were once performed manually by the employee have been replaced by technology. The job role may shift from administrative tasks to more problem-solving and decision-making activities. If those tasks are not identified, the employee will extend the time it takes to perform the remaining tasks. The individual within the new role may no longer be a good fit, and not have the required behaviors to fulfill the role.

The organization may need to examine and change the performance appraisal to include the new standards. New operational policies and procedures may need to be created. The staffing level required will most likely need to change to reflect the new performance standards.

Information and Knowledge Management: Just because the new software application is capable of integrating and automating workflow does not mean that the data used in the transactions is complete and accurate. Additional information or data clean-up may be required to ensure the processing is accurate. Employees need visibility to the right information at the right time, in the right format to make informed decisions. This means that there must be a mechanism to access the information and interpret what the data is saying. To aid in this process, analytic tools and dashboards are used. This may require even more training and understanding of the downstream implications of their decisions. The knowledge that each employee group and individual needed to perform their job must be shared so that one person or group does not withhold valuable information. A knowledge management system, process, and culture must be developed to ensure employees are supporting the organizational goals and values.

16

Information – The Lifeblood of Business

"Information's pretty thin stuff unless mixed with experience."

— Clarence Day

INFORMATION IS THE lifeblood of a business. It is not your product or service; because those are things that you provide based upon the information you obtain from your customers and their needs. Every employee needs information to make informed decisions whether it is ordering hot dogs from a food cart or launching nuclear weapons on enemy positions. However, often business leaders rely on software applications to process the information rather than ensuring the information meets specific quality standards. Wrong information is worse than no information at all. In order for employees to make informed decisions, the information must meet quality standards. Here are ten characteristics that I have found to improve the quality of information that enables employees to make informed decisions that will add value to the business.

1. It must be relevant
2. It must also be clear
3. There must be sufficient accuracy
4. The information must be complete
5. The information must also be trustworthy
6. It must be concise
7. Information must be provided in a timely manner
8. It must be communicated to the right person
9. It must also be communicated via the right channel
10. Information must be less costly than the value it provides

Employees must be able to trust that the information that they are provided will meet quality characteristics defined by the customer to meet their expectations and those of the business. There are many examples where million dollar contracts were lost due to an improper date change, not meeting a critical specification, or failing to meet other specific requirements.

The quality of the information is just one variable to make informed decisions. Employees must have sufficient knowledge or experience to understand what information is valuable, and how to use the data properly. A great example can be found from the Hubble Space telescope that was launched in 1990. Built by the United States space agency NASA, with contributions from the European Space Agency, the 2.4-meter aperture telescope was nearly a failure. In the rush to get the project done on schedule, the sub-contractor skipped a step that through the calibration off 1 millimeter. That critical step caused the reflective mirror to be out of focus equivalent to over 1 mile that made it inoperable. Astronauts had to be specially trained and special tools designed to make the costly repairs in space.

Individual employees often gather their data to be able to perform their job more effectively. That information is often collected on Excel spreadsheets maintained on desktop computers unable to be shared with others within the organization. Soon, there are multiple spreadsheets maintained by many employees. This places the organization at considerable risk for a number of reasons.

1. The individual employee has valuable information that only they are managing. If that individual leaves the organization, that information may end up going with that employee or is lost forever.
2. Others do not share information within the organization. Employees that share the same customer may not have current information.
3. Research Reports state that up to 90% of all Excel spreadsheets contain some errors in their calculation.

Here is a short article recently posted by Fortune magazine: "We should have seen the financial crisis coming. Back in 2003, the giant mortgage guarantor made an error in an Excel spreadsheet when transitioning to a new accounting regulation. The result: an error that made Fannie Mae look $1.3 billion more profitable than it actually was. The company was forced to re-state its results later."

Then there was this story. "About a year before MF Global went bust, consultants hired by the firm determined it needed to improve the "end user computer tools such as Excel spreadsheets" that the commodities broker used to monitor risk and how much money it had in its customers' accounts, and to make sure that some of that money didn't end up in the account being used by CEO Jon Corzine to bet on whether or not Europe was about to implode. Those upgrades were never made."

Employees end up turning to Excel spreadsheets because often they do not have access to enterprise-wide software tools that have the level of sophistication and access to shared databases. It is much easier to generate a spreadsheet quickly than to grant access to available systems. Some managers may resist stating the need and the cost, but citing these examples, it would have been much cheaper than to risk their business.

17

THE THREE LEVELS OF NEED

*"Our most important stakeholder is not our stockholders; it is
our customers. We're in business to serve the needs and desires of
our core customer base."*

— JOHN MACKEY

I RECENTLY RECEIVED A letter from the street department from my town
telling me about a project that they were about to undertake that would
greatly affect me. The letter described how they planned to put in a sidewalk
on my property. In order to do so, they would have to remove a walkway that
extends from my house to the street, a large tree, several bushes, and my entire
driveway. My house is located at the edge of my town and certainly does not
have high pedestrian foot traffic. Their plan was to connect the sidewalk that
currently ended at my neighbor's property to the sidewalk across the street. At
the same time, they plan to install a sidewalk on the opposite side of the street,
removing two large trees in the process.

The supervisor from the street department showed up at my door a few days later to discuss the project. It was only two years ago that the street department removed a section of sidewalk and planted grass, the same piece that they wanted to connect now. I also had a large tree in the proposed path that they decided to keep and work around. I could not see the purpose of this massive undertaking when there was no real need for the public and the added expense. The only reason the supervisor gave me was that there was a plan to connect all of the sidewalks in the town. He could tell that I was not pleased with the plan. To satisfy me, the supervisor told me that it would be a benefit to me because I would get a new driveway, something that I did not need.

This story reminded me of how we approach major change in organizations. Employees observe minor changes that go on throughout the year that are minor disruptions. These small changes are rarely announced and seem to have no real purpose. There may be some speculation where assumptions are made, and employees move on to their daily routine. Then a major change is announced with full fanfare. The communication describes all of the new features and advantages that the change will bring. However, features and functionality are not viewed as a benefit until there is perceived value on the part of the stakeholder. As in the story of the new sidewalk, the supervisor was describing the perceived benefit that a new driveway would be for me.

We should recognize the three levels of need for change. The first level is referred as latent need or pain. A latent need is where the stakeholder does not see the need for change. This type of need can fall into two categories: the stakeholder is ignorant of the potential value that the change can bring, or the stakeholder has concluded that the change is too complicated or too cumbersome to make the effort.

The next level is known as the pain or active need. The stakeholder recognizes a need or pain. They are often anxious to resolve the problem and may be willing to participate actively in the project or will be the change champion to support the initiative.

The third level is known as the vision. The stakeholder understands the vision for the change and will be actively involved in taking responsibility for solving the problem and see the problem being acted upon. Caution should be taken to manage assumptions and expectations. If the vision for change is not fully communicated or if the results of the change initiative are not recognized, then the stakeholder will lose trust in the leadership and may even resist additional efforts.

As I reflect on my sidewalk story, I can see many similarities to the way we manage change at work. The removal of the small piece of sidewalk two years ago was witnessed by me but never explained. I made the assumption that there would never be a sidewalk reinstalled, and for this reason I was relieved that I would have my privacy. The reason unbeknown to me was that the sidewalk did not comply with ADA standards and rather than risk a potential lawsuit; the section was removed.

The replacement of my driveway was not a benefit to me until I perceived it as a value, otherwise it was just a feature and an added advantage to the town workers to keep the sidewalk at a consistent level. Since I had a large crack in the cement driveway, and the town would replace the drive for free, it became a benefit.

I was not aware of the town's long-term plan to connect all of the sidewalks in town. By making me, aware of this plan would aid in resolving my concern over the added expense. I also later had learned that the roads and the curbs were also part of the plan to renovate the public access areas. If I had been aware of the vision from the time I was notified, I would have accepted the proposed change much easier. Instead, for several days after my initial notification I was complaining to my neighbors of the disregard for our tax dollars. I was at level one and ignorant of the perceived value of my property and the town.

Although I still have some assumptions about the timing of the work and expectations of the quality, I am now in favor of the change which is defined as level two - the active need for the change. There may not be a need for me to be at the third level since I do not need to be actively involved in supporting the renovation that is unless my expectations for quality are not achieved. Then I will be actively complaining to the town council. For now, I am thinking positive and with a bit of caution, I support the plan.

18

WHEN TECHNOLOGY IS THE
WRONG SOLUTION

*"Humanity is acquiring all the right technology for all the
wrong reasons."*

— RICHARD BUCKMINSTER FULLER

JUST BECAUSE YOU have the technology to do something does not mean
you should do it. This is what I thought when I went to donate blood
at my local center. A week prior to my appointment I received an email
from the blood donation center telling me all of the new changes that were
implemented to make my experience easier and more enjoyable. They stated
that the screening questions were now all on-line, and I could answer the 50
questions from the convenience of my home. There were other features that
they boasted such as fingerprint recognition to verify who I am and a check
in station at the front door.

The morning of my donation, I went on-line and completed my questionnaire. Upon completion, it had me print the results that were in the form of a bar code. I thought to myself, why would it be necessary to print this information since it is already on their secure website? Upon arriving at the donation center, there was a kiosk situated at the front door. I could see the technicians sitting waiting for me in the room. The computer screen gave me the option to either enter my name and identification number that was printed on my donation card or I could use the scanner to read the barcode. I chose to use the barcode scanner. Placing the card under the scanner I heard a beep, but nothing happened, so I tried it again with the same results. Frustrated, I chose to manually type in my name. By this time, the technician walked over to see what was wrong and patiently waited until the information was entered. Then, she directed me over to a screening room where she asked my name. I handed her the card, and she proceeded to scan it. After verifying my name and address, she performed the preliminary testing of my vital signs then prepared me to answer the 50 questions. I pulled out my printed copy and handed it to her. I thought this was going to save me time. After several attempts to scan the barcode, she gave up in frustration and told me that I would have to answer the questions again. I have been donating blood on a regular basis, at the same location for several years. Every time the question asks if I was in the United Kingdom between 1976 and 1986. The answer is no and will continue to be no, so why keep asking me? There is also what I believe to be a trick question that asks if I am pregnant? You cannot fool these guys. Once complete, the technician reentered the room to review my responses and had me sign an electronic signature pad that was behind me on the desk. That is where I noticed the fingerprint device. When I inquired about this, the technician stated that it was not working. Finally, the screening process is over and the computer prints out a barcode to put on the vials and collection bag, but nothing for me. The technician escorts me across the room to the donation chair, scans the bar code on her handheld device and asks my name again.

With all of the new technical capabilities, was the process more efficient? Did the new functionality make for a satisfying experience? The answer to both questions was a resounding no! I walked away feeling frustrated and angry. Instead of the technician greeting me at the door, they watched while I tried to use the kiosk. Later, I found out that the kiosk was only used to confirm the appointment.

Their computer systems were not smart enough to remember my history and only ask me questions that were relevant to my recent health, and it certainly should know if I am male or female. With intelligent systems, the list of questions would be dramatically reduced and eliminate the need to complete the questions at home and risk the possibility that the bar code readers would not work. Then biometric readers would eliminate the need to carry donation cards and improve patient tracking and quality control. So I go back to my original statement, just because you have the technology to do something does not mean you should do it. The result is that it did not improve the quality, reduce risk, or improve customer satisfaction. Senior leaders should ask themselves what is the business problem that we are trying to solve and how will we know that it has been achieved, then and only then should plans be made to make changes in the process and technology to accomplish those objectives.

19

DRIVING VALUE THOUGH
BUSINESS PROCESSES

*"The system is that there is no system. That doesn't mean we
don't have a process. Apple is a very disciplined company, and
we have great processes. But that's not what it's about. Process
makes you more efficient."*

— STEVE JOBS

A MAJOR TELECOMMUNICATIONS PROVIDER made the decision to enhance
many of their back and front office operations by replacing their existing
software applications with an enterprise-wide, integrated system. The senior
leaders had recognized the problems faced by the organization for many years.
Their existing systems were old and through many customizations were no
longer supported by the software vendor. They also saw the need to share
data between various systems, to reduce errors, and time taken by the dupli-
cation of information. Enhanced analytics and reporting were also sought to

improve problem-solving and the quality of decisions. The leaders also knew that they wanted more than just to replace the software; rather they wanted to improve the business processes that were supported by the software.

One of the requirements that the senior leaders sought was to have the software vendor provide information about the processes that the applications supported. After several meetings to determine the requirements, the vendor was hired to manage the project. Process documents including detailed process maps were provided to the business leaders that identified specific software modules and how they would be used to enhance the process. Although the process documentation satisfied the business leaders and the requirements of the contract, they only served as reference material. There were several issues with the process documentation in its current form:

- The process narratives and maps described in generic terms how information flowed through the process at the functional level.
- Starting at such a detailed level, the process maps did not display wherein the overall value chain where the transactions were taking place.
- The end-to-end workflow through the organization was not illustrated leaving the employees to assume where the output would go, and the requirements needed for the next step.
- Decision and control points were not indicated in the process maps or narratives showing how the operational policies and business rules regulated the process.

It was important to the project that the process documents reflect the desired future state prior to the software application to be configured. How could the project team adequately configure the software to meet the business requirements if they only had the transactional requirements? This is akin to driving across country without the aid of a map but just armed with the description of what the destination looked like once you arrived.

Using the value chain, which is a very high-level diagram of how workflows through the organization from end-to-end, we determined which links in the chain would be impacted by the project. Then we gathered and re-viewed the applicable business policies and rules to understand better what was required to conform. Then, we held group discussions to identify high-level business requirements, current issues, and opportunities. With the in-formation at hand, we mapped the current state to identify how work was actually performed including work around tasks. Using the features and functionality of the new software, along with best practices, we created a fu-ture state design. This new design will assist the technical team to configure the application. Comparing the current and future state processes, we then can identify the gaps which will aid in determining newly assigned tasks, new competencies to learn, new metrics or measures, and even which policies need to be changed or eliminated.

Starting from a strategic viewpoint allows the leaders and project team members to better understand where the change is taking place and the areas that may be influenced by the change in other areas. Using a top-down view of the change helps people to understand and accept the change leading to a smooth and quick adoption that in turn will aid in meeting the project time-frame. We have also learned that the process becomes more efficient, not just through the technology but by eliminating or reducing non-value-added tasks and potential disconnects in the workflow.

20

SUSTAINING THE CHANGE

"People don't resist change. They resist being changed!"

— PETER SENGE

AFTER NEARLY A year of disruption of the business, the project is finally complete, and the new system is live. Project leaders have completed their implementation and have called it a success. Now what…

Business unit leaders are now feeling the effects of the change. There is now a backlog of work to get accomplished due to the conversion of the old application to the new. In addition, overall performance is down. Employees who were very comfortable navigating around the old software are struggling even though they received training. Some of the employees' state their work routine had been disrupted and many of the non-system related activities are now different. Stress levels are high not only among the staff employees but also at the management level where pressure is placed on them to "get things back to normal". What happened, what if anything went wrong? If change management was an active part of the project, why would the organization not be prepared to get back to business?

Many change management activities that are performed during the project are intended to ensure that the project is completed successfully, meaning on-time, within budget, and with an expected level of quality. During the project, the stakeholders were identified, and the leaders were coached. The communication plan provided information in a timely fashion, issues of resistance were managed, individuals were trained just in time, and we celebrated and rewarded effort. Those activities were based upon the many of the popular change management approaches to align the individual employee to the change initiative. As a result of performing these activities, the employees who were most impacted by the change were kept informed of the changes that were to take place; their level of interest was raised, and naysayers were handled. Then these employees underwent training right before the system went live to ensure they remembered how to navigate and use the new application.

None of the change management activities that were performed during the project were conducted to reinforce change. If the change was viewed as just implementing a new tool, then the application training may be all that is needed. It may take several months before the employees are completely proficient in using the new application.

However, a project of this magnitude is often driven by a business problem that requires a change in behaviors. Automated workflow, collaboration, and integration change the way employees perform their jobs and interfaces with others. The effects of the new system will improve the quality of the information, as well as the processing speed. For this reason, job roles may need to be redesigned to adjust the job competencies and performance requirements. The job activities may also shift from administrative tasks to more decision-making and problem-solving. These activities require new behaviors to be effective.

The business process activities and tasks will change due to the increased functionality and features that were implemented in the software application.

Existing policies, work steps, and procedures will most likely be changed or eliminated. New performance metrics and measures may be needed based on the changes.

These activities need not be performed after the project is completed, but rather can be part of an integrated solution. The software applications and other technical functionality can drive a defined level of operational performance. There is also a defined level of performance from well-qualified employees, a well-coordinated organizational structure, from efficient business processes and sound information and knowledge management framework. There is an interdependency between all of these performance drivers that can enhance the overall outcome. By approaching the change initiative from the top down and bottom up, we can achieve the overall objective to enhance the business operation.

21

THE POLITICS IN
ORGANIZATIONAL CHANGE

"He who rejects change is the architect of decay. The only human institution which rejects progress is the cemetery."

— HAROLD WILSON

POLITICS IS MOST apparent when change is mooted and when is there not change these days? Managers need high-level political skills to deal competently with open and covert opposition to change. This might take the form of people agreeing to change in words, but not in action, forming cliques or going slow.

Organizational politics is almost inevitable, but they can be either constructive or destructive. The best management skills would seek to ensure that constructive uses, such as attraction of resources or changed working practices, are delivered by using supportive political skills. The worst skills are tantamount to bullying and dishonesty, which should not be condoned.

Political behavior plays a more significant role in organizational life than is often recognized, or openly admitted. We like to think of our social and organizational cultures as characterized by order, rationality, openness, collaboration, and trust. The reality, however, is often different. Competition sits alongside cooperation. Informal 'back staging' supports public action.

Political maneuvering has been very apparent among mid-level managers than among those at higher or lower levels within the organization. The mid-level manager is often caught between trying to execute the plans derived from those in senior leadership positions while satisfying the needs and maintaining a sense of order among those subordinate.

During my consulting career, I have encountered: self-interest, deceit, deception, and cunning, as well as the pursuit of moral ideals and high aspirations in the name of change. In order to recognize why politics occurs particularly during the change, it is helpful to understand typical reactions to change, such as denial, ignoring the change and self-doubt.

During the change, the emotional climate can be both volatile and fast-moving, especially in the early stages. Later on during changes, some groups will start to benefit from the change and some will perceive they are losing out. As a result, the person or group may take action to preserve that power or even enhance their standing among others.

It is uncommon to see individuals take a stand against the change initiative after it has been sanctioned by the senior leaders. Rather individuals and groups will take a more covert approach to resisting the change. Some of the more common tactics used to delay or stop the initiative include:

- Being slow to respond to requests for information, or not providing complete information.
- Making decisions that only benefit the individual or group and not the organization at large.
- Not being available and actively participate in the change initiative

- Sabotaging the hardware, software, or the data.
- Making vague, misleading statements or inconsistent statements.

It is understandable that there will be resistance to change; some negative behaviors will be more pronounced in some individuals and groups than others. As a result, the level and duration of the resistance will vary. However, how do we tell if the resistance is based upon a political agenda? First we must understand what politics is – simply it is the science of influencing people to a point of view. In an organization, an individual or group may desire to have power, influence and control over a portion of the business. The change initiative may be viewed as a threat that often results in some form of resistance.

Dealing with political issues is more than just winners and losers, but rather reaching an understanding of the various points of view. Often the issues revolve around the characteristics of the job or position such as the span of control, autonomy, variety, significance, the individual basis of power, independence, and the ability to achieve individual goals.

There are times, although not often when there are philosophical differences between an individual employee and the organization. These are differences in the core values that the individual and organization hold. The core values of an organization are those values that we hold which form the foundation on which we perform work and conduct ourselves. We have many values but some of them are so primary and so important to us that throughout the changes in business, technology, and society, they remain the central core of what we value and abide by. In an ever-changing work, core values are consistent. Core values are not descriptions of the work we do or the strategies that we employ to accomplish our mission. The values underlie our work, how we interact with each other, and how we perform our work.

Employees can slowly deviate from the organization's core values by placing priorities over values. A worker may be pressured to skip an inspection in order to ship the product on time. A promise of a promotion may be used to look the other way. Or ignoring customer satisfaction because of increased work demands may cause employees to lose sight of the organization's core values.

Therefore, when the change is based around reinforcing the core values of the organization, employees can rally around a common point of view. Communicating the change in these terms can help decrease resistance to change. However, if there is a difference in core values between the organization and the individual, then there is no longer a good job fit.

22

THE CHANGING ROLE OF
CHANGE MANAGEMENT

"Don't manage - lead change before you have to."

— JACK WELCH

WHAT IS THE value of organizational change management within a major initiative? Before we can determine the significance of managing the "people" change, we need first to look at the overall value of the project itself.

The pace of change is rapidly accelerating; it is especially visible to us in the products we use every day like our cell phone, tablet computer, and our televisions. Business software applications, receive patches and updates on a regular basis. I constantly have to update the applications on my IPad; the same applies to business apps. There is a point where the software vendor will release a new version and will no longer support prior releases. Currently, that cycle time is between three to five years. From the CIO point of view, that application needs to be replaced to maintain licensing agreements and vendor support. The operational business leaders require greater reporting capabilities as well as the elimination of manual work steps through automation. From the CFO viewpoint, he requires a reduction of operating expenses. A strong business case is made to defend the new functionality of the upgraded software while satisfying the needs of these leaders. It is much easier to support a tangible product due to its features and functionality rather than a more abstract work process or behavior.

With the technology being the driver of the change initiative, the goal of organizational change management is to accelerate the acceptance and adoption of the organizational change while minimizing the impact on the day to day operations.

Achieving this change management goal will certainly contribute to the success of the project by meeting timelines and budget projections. Maintaining consistent operational performance levels throughout the project and after the new application goes live also provides value.

However, there are several assumptions that have been made and are seldom verified:

Assumption 1: The organizational culture is such that employees will resist change to some degree which will most likely cause delays in effective problem-solving and making quality decisions.

Assumption 2: Workforce competency levels are high and that nearly all employees have the knowledge, skills, and abilities to perform their current job duties at acceptable levels.

Assumption 3: The current business processes function at near-peak performance and only limited by the constraints of the current technology. The new technology will only enhance the process.

Assumption 4: Communication for change is different from other forms of internal communication and must come from the change management team associated with the project. The primary difference is that change communication addresses changes in behavior and associated risks. Corporate communication is mainly key messages that highlight the features and new capabilities.

Decisions regarding the project are made based upon these assumptions that will ultimately affect the outcome of the change initiative. For this reason, a defensive culture, an insufficiently skilled workforce, ineffective business processes and poor communication and collaboration skills that exist will just be carried forward. The traditional change management activities such as stakeholder mapping, leadership alignment, communication plans, resistance management plans, and so forth will have a limited success. More importantly, these change management activities serve to support the anticipated value of the features and functionality of the new software.

The technology by design will change the KPI's or Key Performance Indicators (quality) and SLA's or Service Level Agreements (time) in the business operation it performs. For example: Let's say that the new software application is integrated with other systems and databases and provides automated workflow to various employees. The data that is shared with other systems eliminates the need for manual and duplicate entry of information, thereby reducing the amount of errors resulting in improved quality. The automated workflow reduces the time to deliver the information to the next person. Some systems will also forward the action to the next person if no action is taken within a defined period. For this reason, the service level to process the action is reduced saving time.

Eliminating administrative work steps, shortening time frames, and improving the level of quality will require a change in the business processes and competency levels of the position. Therefore, organizational change management must include an organizational culture component to change the behaviors of employees, an organizational development component to change the job requirements and position competency levels, and an organizational effectiveness component to determine new performance metrics and measures.

By adding these additional activities added value, can be achieved by the people and process side, as well as those functions enabled by the new technology. The change will have a lasting effect that extends far beyond the current project.

23

TRUST – IS TELECOMMUTING EFFECTIVE

"When people honor each other, there is a trust established that leads to synergy, interdependence, and deep respect. Both parties make decisions and choices based on what is right, what is best, what is valued most highly."

— BLAINE LEE

RECENTLY YAHOO'S CEO Marissa Mayer made national news by announcing that she will put an end to telecommuting within her company citing the need for a physical presence with coworkers to develop a need to share ideas and to be more productive. This created an uproar especially among working moms who struggle with maintaining a work-life balance.

Google, Apple, and Facebook encourage face-to-face collaboration though they do not openly discourage telecommuting. Indeed, most tech companies do not have formal policies -- it usually is a mix of working onsite and at home, based on the project and managers involved.

In a Forbes article published September 19, 2012, they stated that research conducted at Stanford with a Chinese company revealed that working from home is actually more productive than working in the office – and had other benefits in the form of increased job satisfaction and decreased job turnover. They also discovered that home workers' productivity soared by 13% over their office counterparts. On investigation, 9.5% of the increase in productivity was shown that employees that work from home put in more hours. They started on time, unhampered by a delayed commute; they took fewer breaks (less gossiping at the water cooler) and had fewer days off sick. The other 3.5% productivity increase was because they took more calls per minute. Their quiet working environment allowed them to concentrate more – a fact that anyone who's tried to take a business call while teammates loudly discuss last night's game can sympathize.

Many managers still hold the belief that they must "manage" the actions of their subordinates. To have this control, these managers must be able to monitor tasks and be available for decisions that need to be made. This style is a throwback from the management style of the 1950's where control through micro management was the norm. The primary reason may be due in part to the economic conditions that are facing organizations to do more with less.

Here are some truths that should help clarify this issue:

- Managers need to learn to become leaders of employees by creating an environment of trust and support. Managers should, therefore, manage work processes by eliminating obstacles for their employees.
- Not all people can be trusted to telecommute; they simply need structure and control in their lives. This does not make them less valued as an employee, but rather need defined roles and tasks. Telecommuting is great for disciplined, self-motivated people who can work in an environment where there is little structure and can work toward self-set goals.
- Not all jobs lend themselves to telecommuting. Some jobs require a physical presence of the employee to perform their tasks effectively.

Also, some organizations just do not have the maturity level of their business processes, technology, or their culture to support and sustain an effective telecommute environment.

For right now, the issue is trust. Can management trust their employees to carry out their assigned duties to attain a desired level of performance and quality? Likewise, can employees trust that management will stand behind them when difficult decisions were made? Trust is defined as a firm reliance on the integrity, ability, or character of a person. It is the assured reliance on the character, strength, ability, or truth of someone in which confidence is placed. Mutual trust is a shared belief that you can depend on each other to achieve a common purpose. Trust is more than just your attitude toward someone; it has a direct impact on the business operation and the success of an initiative. Listed below are benefits of creating trust:

Increased Efficiency -- As team members trust that everyone will carry out her responsibility, all can attend their specific functions more completely. The decrease in distractions gives an increase in efficiency.

Enhanced Unity -- The greater each member of a team trusts other members, the greater strength the team assumes. This unity strengthens the team's commitment to fulfilling its purpose.

Mutual Motivation -- When two (or more) people trust one another, each one consciously and subconsciously strives to uphold the others' trust. That motivation stimulates each team member to seek peak performance.

Creating trust takes a strong adaptive constructive organizational culture. When the organization is structured in a way that promotes collaboration; When jobs are designed with greater autonomy; When policies are used as guidelines rather than strict rules more important than ideas; and when goals are mutually set and rewarded will trust become a core value.

24

ADAPTIVE SKILLS FOR CHANGE

"We now accept the fact that learning is a lifelong process of keeping abreast of change. And the most pressing task is to teach people how to learn."

— PETER DRUCKER

THE KEY TO a successful organization lies in its ability to be innovative and adapt to change without hindering that organization's overall operation. Often an organization will exhaust too many of its resources trying to adopt quick fixes for things that have gone wrong. By becoming trapped in this cycle of "fixing," an organization is no longer moving forward. This can lead to serious problems such as increased turnover, decreased morale and ineffective communication. By definition, an Adaptive Culture is simply a way of operating where change is expected and adapting to those changes is smooth, routine and seamless. With an Adaptive Culture in place, change, growth and innovation are a "given" part of the business environment.

Given an increased need for people to be adaptable in their jobs when faced with operational change, the first question to ask is "what does it mean to be adaptable?" Adaptability is an effective change in response to an altered situation. There are three main points to know about this definition. First, behavior change is at the core of the definition. Persisting in a course of action despite environmental changes is not adaptive – even if it is effective. In other words, continuing to do what one has been doing is not a display of adaptability. Second, the change that is made must be effective. It is not adaptive to make a change that makes it more difficult to reach a goal or takes one further from a desired end-state. To be adaptable, the change that is made must work. Third, the change must be a response to some shift in the work environment. Changing one's behavior in a random whimsical fashion is not adaptive. Rather adaption arises from the situation and environmental changes.

There are seven dimensions of adaptability that describe different kinds of adaptive behavior that might be displayed. These dimensions are as follows:

- Handling crisis situations as a result of the change
- Handling work stress in the face of change
- Solving problems creatively and effectively
- Dealing effectively with unpredictable or changing work situations
- Learning new work tasks, technologies, and procedures
- Demonstrating interpersonal adaptability
- Adapting to different leadership styles and goals due to a merger or acquisition.

For simplicity sake for managing change during a major initiative, we can group these into two overarching types of adaptability.

- Mental adaptability – Being mentally adaptable means adjusting one's thinking in new situations to overcome obstacles or improve the effectiveness. It includes things like handling crisis situations, handling stress, learning new things, and creative problem-solving.

- Interpersonal Adaptability – Being interpersonally adaptable means adjusting what one says and does to make interactions with other people run more smoothly and effectively. This includes trying to understand the needs and motives of other people especially when new ideas, concepts, and approaches are used.

Now that we have a better understanding of adaptability, the change management practitioners can now address these two types of adaptability issues by showing how stakeholders can use tools and techniques to guide them through a change process.

Mental adaptability – focuses on ways in which people must adjust their thinking to handles change effectively. The stakeholders will need to focus on their ability to recognize and adjust to changes by switching mindsets as necessary by thinking critically and using a structured problem-solving approach.

One suggestion is to introduce the six-step problem-solving process.

The problem for most stakeholders is that they do not use one process to solve problems to make quality decisions. Another problem is that they are not consistent in how to solve problems. The six-step problem-solving process is an easy approach to identify systematically, diagnose and generate solutions and not get bogged down in what to do next. Here are the steps:

1. Identify and select the problem by creating a problem statement.
2. Analyze the problem by mapping out the process, listing the steps, and identifying the potential root causes.
3. Generate potential solutions to solve the problem.
4. Select the most appropriate solutions based on the project criteria such as time, cost, resources and other factors.
5. Implement the solution by testing it out on a small scale to determine if it meets the requirements.
6. Evaluate the result by measuring the results and determining improvements.

Interpersonal adaptability – focus on the ways in which people adjust their behaviors depending on the social demands of a situation. There are two parts to this section: helping the stakeholders understand themselves and how they understand and interact with others.

Understanding of oneself – using the DISC model, or MBTI assessment to understand one's personality styles within various social situations. Understanding one's personality type can bring insight to an individual's strengths and weakness, and how they interact within a group environment.

Understanding others – Stakeholders can use collaborative tools and techniques to understand differing points of view better to gain consensus on the changes. The six-step problem-solving process can promote collaboration. Using tools such as criteria rating forms, list reduction, point scoring, weighted voting and other tools when using the structured-solving process can aid in building adaptive skills for a successful change. As the stakeholders work through the process with the tools, they learn about differing viewpoints and build consensus and commitment to the change.

25

MORE THAN BUSINESS INTELLIGENCE

"B.I. is about providing the right data at the right time to the
right people so that they can take the right decisions."

— NIC SMITH

MANY MATURE ORGANIZATIONS operate in functional silos such as finance, I.T., Sales, procurement, and human resources to centralize control. For the most part, this type of structure is sufficient. However in today's fast-paced, global business, the isolated structure is limited by the real-time information that is required to make informed decisions quickly.

Standardized reports have been used for years for validation, compliance, reporting, and decision-making. There are many flaws in standardized reports: They represent a point in time rather than indicating patterns or trends; these reports show one point of view or one dimension rather than looking at multiple aspects; standard reports generally have a limited audience of managers; the reports have a limited lifespan, meaning that the data can become quickly outdated since it reflects historical information; and creating reports takes a great deal of I.T. resources.

In their desire to quickly give managers reports, some I.T. teams try to anticipate the managers' needs, gather data and create custom reports and dashboards they think the managers will use based upon their past requests. But this approach often fails because I.T. managers don't think like managers of finance, sales, procurement, and human resources. The reports aren't used because they lack the insight those department manger's need or the reports go through multiple revisions to get it "just right." And when the business changes as it invariably will, the reports need to be revised again. Although there still is a need for reports, the need for timely information has evolved into analytic reporting or business intelligence.

An IBM researcher, Hans Peter Luhn coined the phrase Business Intelligence in an article published in 1958. Today, Business Intelligence has evolved into data warehousing and data integration to provide data analysis using powerful analytic tools. These powerful applications can provide the manager with a near real-time view of the business operation. The application allows the user to create custom reports or views with drill around or drill down capabilities. Analytic tools have greatly enhanced the manager's capability to make decisions, but there are still limitations.

Business intelligence needs to be more than just an analytic tool but viewed as a broader philosophy to manage knowledge. Rather than transforming raw data into meaningful and useful information provided to a limited group of managers, a knowledge management approach should be created for all. The organization must work to value the sharing of knowledge. This can be achieved by creating strategies and practices to identify, create, represent, distribute and enable the adoption of insights and experiences. This can be achieved by:

Collaborative work teams: Create teams based on a process rather than functional silos. This will promote the free exchange of information and the open sharing of ideas. Collaboration works to achieve a common goal. When people are involved in the process, they become committed and take ownership.

Access to information: Do not restrict lower level employees to access the information they need that relates to their job function. These frontline employees need information to make quality decisions. Defining data security by roles hampers the ability for employees to see the broader picture.

Map Critical Business Processes: By understanding the value chain, business rules, decision points, and hand-off's employees will perform their work consistently using the same standards and measures. The reporting and analysis will be consistent and will promote better problem-solving and quality decisions.

The business intelligence amounts to getting the right information, faster, to the right people -- who in turn can take the right action, faster, against the right objective. Creating a culture of collaborative knowledge sharing can provide a greater awareness of organizational change. Proponents say that a shared awareness increases synergy for command and control, resulting in superior decision-making and the ability to coordinate complex business operations over long distances for an overwhelming competitive advantage.

26

INFLUENCE AND PERSUASION

"There is no such thing as a good influence. Because to influence a person is to give him one's own soul. He does not think his natural thoughts or burn with his natural passions. His virtues are not real to him. His sins, if there is such a thing as sins, are borrowed. He becomes an echo of someone else's music, an actor of a part that has not been written for him."

— OSCAR WILDE

BUSINESS LEADERS ARE placed in a position to influence change within their organization. But often that becomes a difficult obstacle to overcome. There seems to be a comfort level among employees attained over time where work activities are performed in a routine. Employees will develop behaviors and expectations to fit in, and be accepted by the organization or the work group.

When change is introduced to that routine, and the expectations are altered, then resistance is felt. Whatever the driver of the change, business leaders are hopeful they can influence employees that the change is beneficial to them and their organization. The expectation among management often is to get it done quickly, which means to influence employees that the change is beneficial to the business and is a good thing. Once the employees are told of the changes by their superiors, plans are put in place to implement the changes. Timelines are established, project team members are in place, and the transformation begins.

Leaders used their positional power to influence employees to change their attitude of how they feel about the change through top-down communication and directives. They attempt to change the employee's behavior generally through training. Those employees that conform are recognized and allowed to continue. Those employees who resist are punished and will eventually be removed.

Some leaders are good at persuading employees to embrace the change and make the transition. How is it that some leaders have a difficult time influencing employees to change while other leaders can use their power of persuasion to achieve the desired behavioral results?

Influence and persuasion are often used interchangeably; however we need to start with a deeper understanding of their definition. Influence is a catch-all term. Whenever you attempt to deliberately direct or change a person's thoughts, feeling or behaviors, then influence is said to have occurred. Persuasion, on the other hand, is a subset of Influence. It is when you use communication to try and deliberately change a person's attitude.

There is a subtle but important meaning in the use of the words. Both terms are concerned with deliberate change, but they are different in that persuasion requires a certain level of communication such that an attitude change in adopted by the person. This communication is likely to be a combination of verbal and non-verbal messages. Influence, on the other hand, can be achieved without any communication. It is directed at the person to achieve a specific behavior change without any interaction or effort.

Influence occurs when one's emotions, opinions, or behaviors are affected by others. In a change initiative, this social type of influence can take on many forms and can be seen in conformity, socialization, peer pressure, and obedience from positional power, or fear of reprisal such as the loss of a job, status, or position.

However, it is far better to manage change through inclusion rather than exclusion. Persuasion involves a close interaction and sharing of opinions among people. Although persuasion takes more effort, the results are more favorable and lasting.

Creating an open dialog is essential in persuading employees to embrace the change. Identify and diagnose their issues and concerns. Then explore the impact that the change will have on the individuals and other groups. Once their concerns have been identified, the next step is to help them visualize the capabilities of the change. Solicit the employee's input to solve their concern while helping them visualize the benefits of the change initiative. Confirm the employees understanding of the solution to create a vision of the change that they can embrace. Once mastered, persuasion can be a powerful tool in your change management toolkit.

27

COMMUNICATION FOR LEARNING

"To effectively communicate, we must realize that we are all different in the ways we perceive the world and use this understanding as a guide to our communication with others."

— Tony Robbins

E MPLOYEES, CUSTOMERS, AND suppliers acquire knowledge through communicating information and ideas. Each group has acquired unique information through their experiences that are shared among themselves. Each group has their own distinctive language that relates to the work that they perform. Ginnie Mae is not the new employee in the finance department but rather a U.S. security, and the I.T. group discusses JAVA, but this is not the hot, bold brew that we all enjoy. Despite these language differences, work somehow gets accomplished. How can these and other groups communicate with each other, let alone exchange important information that will support the business? What price do we pay for missed communication that is needed to sustain the business?

In mature organizations, there is a tendency to operate in a bureaucratic style, where defined procedures, rules, and behavioral expectations dictate how individuals interact and share information. Vertical silos of work groups are formed with defined goals and objectives that may not be consistent with other group's goals. A product team that supports specific customers may not be aware of another product team that has targeted the same customers resulting in competing objectives that will create confusion among the customers.

Groups often do not consider what is important or needed by the other group. Withholding information from others may limit the ability to problem-solve effectively and make informed decisions. When information is determined to be factual, can add value to the business or customer, and repeatable, it becomes knowledge.

Knowledge is defined as "a fluid mix of specific experiences, contextual information, values and expert insight that provides a framework for evaluating and incorporating new experiences and information."

To effectively communicate valuable information that can create, share, and store knowledge throughout the organization requires an adaptive and constructive culture. Behaviors that value and actively support employee satisfaction empowered teams, and collaboration report higher levels of shared knowledge across the organization. Here are some key points to implement:

- **Emphasize the big picture** of what the organization needs to accomplish. Make an effort to articulate the long-term goals that support the vision.
- **Promote active discussions** to enthusiastically communicate learning. In order to fully understand the goals and objectives, people need to express their opinions, concerns and fears openly and their needs in an environment that is safe and free from criticism and reprisals. Create a sense of community where employees can feel relaxed and where brief, informal conversations can take place.
- **Learn from our mistakes**. Nobody likes making mistakes. But, unless you want to go through life as a complete recluse, you are guaranteed to make one every now and then.

- **Taking calculated risks** should be encouraged but can lead to mistakes. If you go through life afraid to make a mistake, you'll spend most of your life doing absolutely nothing.
- **Communication for learning reflects the team perspective.** When we have open communication within a group, we make an interpretation of what is said based on our own experiences and knowledge. When we subsequently use this interpretation to guide decision-making or action, then the meaning of the decision becomes 'learning'.

Not all learning involves 'learning to do'. Of even greater significance to most adult learning is the understanding of the meaning of what others communicate: the concerning values, ideals, feelings, moral decisions, and such concepts as job autonomy, influence, and commitment. The influence and power of the group can influence or control the decisions that are made to improve and learn. These influences can also be so strong that they can alter one's judgment in what they believe is correct. These beliefs and expectations are a direct result of the organization's culture.

28

EMPLOYEE INVOLVEMENT
AND COMMITMENT

"The difference between involvement and commitment is like ham and eggs. The chicken is involved; the pig is committed."

— UNKNOWN AUTHOR

ONE OF THE keys to successful change is to get employees involvement in the change initiative. Their commitment comes when leaders allow the employees to make decisions. Employees will become involved when their interest is peaked mainly by being included in issues that have a direct or indirect impact on their jobs or the organization.

However, employees are often left on the sidelines to be told about the initiative and given a specified timeframe to adapt their work behaviors to the change. As a result, employees resist the change. Leaders mistakenly assume that employees will resist change. The truth is that people adapt to change all the time, they just resist when they do not have control over the change. In some work environments where projects are championed by, and led by management they allow individual employees to take the initiative to be included to achieve some specific goal. It assumes that there is a common interest between employees and management. Its main functions are to elicit and to grow employee identification and commitment. Employee involvement is the process in which management allows or gives permission to employees to participate in an activity. Examples of employee involvement during a change initiative include: mapping current state business processes to identify bottlenecks, disconnects, and non-value added activities; participation in design sessions, participate in end-user testing or being a champion of change within their workgroup.

On the other hand, employee commitment, unlike involvement, is collective. It is an act of sharing in something. It is therefore joining with others in every activity that matters. Commitment carries with it an obligation of a promise to ourselves and others. It requires both a mental and emotional investment to take action and live with the consequences of potential failure. To take on the responsibility and the associated risks and the commitment has to be the community within our workplace, not just to our individual interests or our career. Employees have to be both involved and have the commitment for the sake of both the organization and the individual employee.

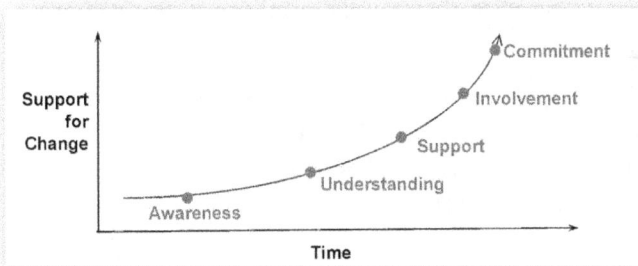

The diagram above illustrates the stages in which employees must go through to achieve commitment. This transition takes time and understanding how each group will foster this support. Having a constructive organizational culture where the workforce is trusted and collaboration exists, the transition through each stage will move swiftly.

Checklist for Securing Employee Involvement and Commitment

1. Does the senior leadership team display a sense of urgency through their actions? This would include: shifting priorities, dedicating resources to the area of concern, and being more involved in the details.
2. Do people at all levels have relevant information that they can place into a meaningful context to take action?
3. The physical work environment has a direct relationship to the ability to communicate. Does your work environment enable teamwork and socialization?
4. Is there a full disclosure of information available to employees to access and use as they may, or is the information filtered, limited, and reserved to the trusted few people?
5. Does the management take the time to understand the issues or roadblocks, and then take action to resolve these issues?
6. Does the organization support and enable the free flow of ideas and information by allowing people the courtesy of time and the forum to have an open communication?
7. Are employees allowed to be involved in making improvements that are supporting the overall change?
8. Is a good attempt that results in failure recognized as a way to learn and grow?
9. Do the employees feel that they are valued by actions and recognition that management takes to keep people involved?
10. Is there sufficient time allowed to transition through each phase of the commitment curve?

29

USING REWARDS AND
PUNISHMENTS FOR CHANGE

*"If you believe in yourself and have dedication and pride - and
never quit, you'll be a winner. The price of victory is high but
so are the rewards."*

— PAUL BRYANT

OUR BASIC STRATEGY for training dogs new tricks, raising children, or managing workers is by offering some type of reward from candy to bonuses to get the favored response that we hope to achieve. This reward is a powerful motivator, and nothing motivates more than success.

I worked to train my dog some basic tricks like to give me his paw and to roll over. We worked on it for a few days. Each time he did it successfully, I gave him a treat. After about a week, he not only mastered the trick, but would perform all of the tricks at once, even before I would give the command. He knew that doing this routine would give him the reward he desired. There was no thinking involved, just a learned behavior that pleased me and achieved an immediate response.

My friend started to reward his children for getting an "A" on their report card. He offered them fifty dollars for each superior mark they achieved. The kids were thrilled with the possibility of receiving a maximum amount of $250.00 for all five classes in that grading period. However, that experiment did not last that long. Five months of school work was too much for the kids to keep them motivated. They liked the idea of receiving money but knew it was not needed since their parents would provide for them.

In business, we use various rewards to help motivate employees. Our sales force will receive commissions on the products and services they sell and give bonuses to support personnel for meeting performance targets. Some managers use various types of recognition for rewarding employees such as giving time off for working extra hours on a special project, being publically recognized for employment milestones, or given a certificate of achievement for their dedication.

Nothing motivates more than success. Extrinsic rewards such as money, certificates, or public recognition work for some people, while intrinsic rewards such as being able to accomplish challenging goals, work with and help others, and having the choice to choose what you do will motivate others. Success is, therefore, a personal perception and should be understood before a recognition or reward is offered.

Rewards are great motivators to change behaviors. However, rewards have limitations. Not all people are motivated by the same thing. Public recognition for good performance may intimidate some or make them feel singled out over others who may have worked just as hard. Not everyone is motivated by money. Some people say that the money is not worth the time and aggravation that the work may entail. The effectiveness of the reward has a half-life. Bonuses and commissions for achieving a level of work performance or changing behavior will only last for a period of a year. Employees will start to expect the added income as part of their regular compensation and will lose the enticement that it was meant to produce. Therefore, create short term goals and use a variety of rewards.

The use of rewards is a short term motivator and is an important tool in the Organizational Change Management practitioner's bag of tools. The use of rewards helps to buy time while the systems and structures are developed and put into place. Once established, the new behaviors become the standard acceptable culture within the organization. Those that do not conform to the new standard will need to be punished. This may sound harsh, but people need to understand that there are consequences for their actions. Take, for example, the seat belt laws. Everyone is expected to buckle-up or receive a ticket for violating the rule.

The use of punishment is equally important as the use of reward when trying to change behavior. Although people have the option to participate in a rewards program, they cannot opt out of participating in the change and conforming to the new behavior. Therefore, communicate to everyone the desired result that the initiative is designed to achieve. Describe how the old ways were hurting the organization and how it affects future business. Focus on the new behaviors in the change communication and describe scenarios how employees changed and made a difference. Tell stories about the benefits and rewards of the new behaviors while not mentioning punishments. When the majority of employees adapt to the new behaviors, then, start to shift the message from rewards to the punishment of non-conformance.

It is important to make sure that the old behaviors are no longer rewarded. To ensure compliance, business policies, rules, and procedures need to be reviewed. Old business processes need to change to ensure that shortcuts and workaround steps are no longer acceptable. Job roles, competencies, and performance review procedures should not encourage or tolerate undesirable behaviors.

There are a number of areas that need to be addressed across: people and organizational systems, business processes, technologies used, and information and knowledge shared to shape and drive the new behaviors that are defined in the change initiative. Recognizing and rewarding the behaviors in these areas will aid in achieving the change vision.

30

ALIGNING ORGANIZATIONAL CULTURE TO SUPPORT CHANGE

"If you don't like change, you will like irrelevance even less."

— GENERAL ERIC SHINSEKI

THE SUCCESS OF a large-scale change initiative and its ability to maintain the organization's competitive advantage is greatly influenced by the organizational culture. It exerts a powerful influence on people's behavior and the decisions they make. What is organizational culture?

Organizational culture includes the standards of behavior within the organization, the invisible rules in which people in the company work, their common beliefs, values, and the expectations they hold. If any change initiative is not compatible with the organizational culture, usually that new practice comes undone over time. Old habits die hard. So change, for it to be lasting must be firmly rooted in the culture of the organization. How can this be achieved? Several actions can help solidify new practices into the existing culture. These are:

- Talking about the issues that are currently faced by the organization. Make sure that people understand the problem that is being faced and the pain that it is causing. Talk about the vision for change. Describe how the organization will operate in the future and how people will feel once it is complete. Then talk about the plan to achieve that goal, the steps that will be taken, and the time frame expected to achieve the goal.
- Identify and remove the barriers that reinforce old, undesirable behaviors. Examine the existing work processes to eliminate unnecessary steps. Examine how people work together and share information across groups and eliminate outdated policies that prevent people from making decisions.
- Tie the results to the changes. Measure the outcomes based on the desired changes and reward the new behaviors.

Communicating the need to change aids in defining the purpose, creating a sense of urgency not only for the organization but the potential impact on employees. These concepts may look something like this: If we continue to delay filling orders, our customers will find a new supplier causing us to go out of business.

Describing a future state vision aids in motivating employees by stating what the leadership team believes is possible. We will have automated systems that will process orders giving employees more time to work with the customer in planning their future needs.

We will start by asking each employee where they see problems exist. Then we will redesign the work processes to standardize tasks and make them more efficient. New technology will be added to automate workflow and provide current information so that employees have the knowledge to do their jobs more effectively.

Then we will measure key points along the process and make that information available to all employees so everyone knows what it will take to achieve our goal.

By doing these things, the culture of the organization will start to shift towards a new adaptive and constructive behavioral style. Integrating systems and automating workflow may provide incremental improvements, but it will not have a noticeable change in the ability of the employees to be innovative and readily adapt to change; effectively problem-solve and achieve quality decisions; have satisfied customers and employees; and consistently provide quality products and services.

Those are the outcomes of the organization's culture, or, in other words, the consequences of their actions. To ensure there is an adaptive and constructive culture, we must look at those principles and values that the employees and the organization considers core to their beliefs. The vision of change may resonate those beliefs, but sustainment is derived from the principle drivers of behavior. Those include: the selection of candidates who have the same values as the organization. Placing that candidate in the most appropriate position that will best utilize their skills and experience; designing jobs that provide greater autonomy; creating an organizational structure that promotes collaboration; policies and practices that reinforce the core values; the appropriate use of recognition and rewards; leadership and managerial styles; open and effective communication both upward and downward; and the ability to set goals for employees that align with the organization.

Combining the people and organizational changes with changes in business process, technology, and knowledge management will ensure a successful change in the organizational culture toward an adaptive and constructive behavior.

There is a wonderful article that was published in the June – July 2012 edition of Harvard Business review entitled _"Cultural Change That Sticks"_ by Jon R. Katzenbach, Ilona Steffen, and Caroline Kronley. The article describes how Aetna Insurance made an organizational culture shift that turned around their business. The story illustrates how addressing culture as part of your transformation can provide dramatic results.

31

COLLABORATIVE PROBLEM-SOLVING

"The problems that exist in the world today cannot be solved by the level of thinking that created them."

— ALBERT EINSTEIN

THINK BACK TO the last time you and your team set out to solve a critical, complex problem. Were the results of your team's effort effective; did it yield the results that you and the others were looking to accomplish; and was it a pleasant experience? If you answered "no" to any or all of these questions, don't feel alone. Many groups struggle to create a viable solution that offers a high degree of value, and an outcome that is accepted and supported by everyone.

A great solution is worthless if the group did not actively participate in the process to create buy-in and support. Likewise, if the group quickly comes to an agreement without properly analyzing the problem or the solution alternatives, then the resulting decision will be of poor quality. The group must work together in an intersection of common goals. This act of people working together constructively to achieve a common purpose is called collaboration.

Collaborative problem-solving is part art and science. To achieve a high-quality solution that is acceptable to the group members requires a collaborative effort, a structured process with well-defined tools, and the knowledge and skill to use them effectively.

There are many approaches to solving a problem, depending upon the nature of the problem and the people who are involved in the problem-solving process. No matter what approach that is used to solve the problem; the goal of this process is the quality of the decision and its acceptance. Characteristics of a quality decision include:

- A collaborative team effort to identify and define both the problem and the solution.
- The acceptance of both the problem and the solution with individuals and the collective group.
- A defined problem-solving process and the standards established and used in the process.
- The synergy of the group to participate and work effectively.
- The rational skills among group members to provide the ability to think clearly and sensibly, unimpaired by personal, political, or cultural prejudices.
- The individual competencies, behaviors, personality and influence of each group member.
- The interpersonal communication skills
- The behavioral styles of the group that are influenced by the operational culture within the organization.

There are a variety of methods and models that are available to project teams. Selecting a process that is easy to use and involves collaboration is preferred. Complex, theoretical models, will quickly diminish group participation. I prefer using a six-step problem-solving process along with a defined set of tools used to generate ideas, and collect information; to analyze and display the data; to reach consensus, and to create plans.

Step 1 – Identify and select the problem: The group develops a statement of the problem that is clearly understood by all members. In addition, the group should develop a statement of the "desired state" to be achieved by solving the problem. Some tools to collect the information include brainstorming, surveys, and interviews. Tools to display the data include Criteria rating forms, criteria matrix, and weighted voting.

Step 2 – Analyze the Problem: Having specified and collected the data necessary to analyze the problem, the group identifies the key cause(s) of the problem. Some tools to analyze the data include cause / effect analysis (Fishbone), Pareto charts, pie charts and time charts.

Step 3 – Generate Potential Solutions: The group produces as many ways as possible -- including some wild ideas -- to solve the problem. Some tools to generate potential solutions are the same as in step one.

Step 4 – Select the Planning Solution: The group decides on the optimum solution and plans its implementation. Some tools that are used to plan the solution include flow charts, Gantt charts, and pert charts.

Step 5 – Implement the Solution: Group members and others are now involved implementation and monitor the solution according to the plan developed in Step 4. A tool used to implement the solution is the check sheet.

Step 6 – Evaluate the Solution: The group learns how effectively their solution solved the identified problem. Some tools that are used to evaluate the solution include the histogram, Pareto Analysis, and scattergrams.

Using a systematic, collaborative approach to solving problems can help the group avoid some of the common pitfalls of ineffective problem-solving. In addition, building a collaborative solution greatly aids in organizational change management to gain acceptance of the initiative.

32

Is Change Management worth it?

"Unless you are prepared to give up something valuable you will never be able to truly change at all because you'll be forever in the control of things you can't give up."

— Andy Law

A SK TEN PEOPLE what organizational change management is, and you are likely to get just as many answers. Then ask those people what value change management provides, and you may get blank stares in return.

Many large-scale change projects have Change Management professionals assigned to support the initiative. Consulting companies provide the project management and technical expertise to guide businesses through the layers of complexity. Change management consultants are part of the project team and have assigned tasks to support the initiative. Certainly, these consulting companies see the value in providing change management, and will devote resources to achieving this goal, but is this the same goal that the organization desires to achieve? So, what are the activities and what value do they bring?

In most cases, the change management activities constitute communication and training to prepare staff members to perform their tasks differently. Certainly these activities are important but do these activities provide equivalent value and comparable worth for the project? Many consulting companies believe so. They use change management to ensure their contracted portion of the project gets implemented smoothly by addressing client concerns and preparing the employees to use the new systems.

Let's examine some change management activities starting with communication. There are two types of communication, the key message and behavioral. **Key Message Communication** is defined as the delivery of any information that does not require action. Any communication for which there is no discernible consequence if the recipient ignores it. **Behavioral Communication** is the delivery of any information, in any form or format, designed to drive a specific action with clearly defined measures, consequences, and rewards. Therefore, key messages raise awareness and understanding of the change. This is an activity that should be the responsibility of the project sponsor, key stakeholders, and other leaders that should be performed as a matter, of course. Why should the communication style and method change or be controlled just because there is a change initiative going on? Frequent and specific dialog should be part of the organization's DNA to promote trust.

What behaviors do we want to change? How should people act differently especially if the project is technology focused? We want the employees to use the new applications and follow the new work steps because of the change. Therefore, the question is, will a message from a change management consultant, yield enough weight, or create the motivation to compel an employee to change their actions? Generally not, a change management consultant can draft the messages and create the communication vehicles to get the message out to the audiences, but do not have the authority to compel others to act. The focus must be on the outcomes of the communication, not the activity.

Training is the other change management activity identified. The question then is: Are organizational change management professionals the best qualified to design or facilitate training? Many OCM practitioners are skilled in facilitation and developing presentations. However, training development and training facilitation are not core competencies, nor would you want to shift the focus of change management away from behavior modification to develop and deliver training. So is this the best value of organizational change management?

I believe that the role of Organizational change management is to assist leaders in transitioning from the current state of behavior to a new desired state regardless of the driver of the change. The business questions should be:

1. What behaviors that currently exist that are creating a problem and need to change?
2. What are the desired new behaviors and why are they important?
3. What barriers prevent employees from acting in the desired way?

So, is change management worth doing? When there is a strong desire to change behaviors of employees to achieve desired outcomes, there is a long-term anticipated effect on the organization that will sustain the change, the answer is a resounding yes. If the goal is to tell employees what the change will be on the organization, then provide training to learn a new task or skill, then the answer must be no. In the latter scenario, there is not a need or desire for change management, but rather the need for competency training.

33

The Great Road Trip

"The stories we tell literally make the world. If you want to change the world, you need to change your story. This truth applies both to individuals and institutions."

— Michael Margolis

L ATE LAST YEAR I was asked to provide change management support for a major insurance company in Chicago. This well-established institution was on firm financial ground due to their risk adverse, conservative management style. Come to think of it, I believe most insurance companies tend to be that way. The organization was highly structured with job roles well defined. Every person had a clearly defined job and clearly knew who was responsible for each task of the claims process.

The new claims processing software that was being implemented offered a great deal of features and functionality that would greatly benefit this large company. The extensive amount of notes that the claims processors took over the telephone were being replaced by on-line forms with an assortment of pre-defined responses allowing for standardization and improved efficiency. There were many other features such as workflow triggers, assignment cues and a host of other functionality that could be configured.

Departments that supported the claims processing were located in various cities across the United States. The task of requirements gathering, configuration, testing, training, and deployment became quite a challenge. The project team was well established when I arrived. Doing a quick assessment, I learned that the planning was already performed and the implementation team was already defining the functional requirements needed to configure the software. The prospect of managing the changes proved to be an equally difficult task in an organization that was set in their ways. I did not have the luxury of taking an active part in the planning phase, rather, I had to play catch-up and work with the information provided.

The Vice-presidents did not want their business units disrupted by the changes taking place. Communication was to be kept to a minimum as they felt that their staff was already receiving too many messages distracting them from their work. In addition, the vision of how the business was going to operate in the future was not clearly defined. The vice-presidents felt the best thing to do, was to communicate the change only after it took place or when the staff members required training.

The software implementation team determined their best way to define the requirements at these remote locations was to use the agile project method. The project was then divided into fourteen phases with each phase to be completed at each location. Only then would they know how the system and the business would operate. My challenge was to develop a way to communicate the change and prepare the organization for the new way to function. After contemplating the limitations and change management needs, I finally came up with a plan.

The great road trip concept was born. As I reflected back when my parents decided to take the family on a vacation, they would always drive. My parents described where we were going, but we did not have a real clear idea what our destination would look like. There would be fourteen stops on our cross country trip. On our way to each destination, we would see and experience new things. Sometimes along our trip there may be slowdowns and even detours. When we would arrive at each stop on our journey, we pick up new things that we treasure, we would take memorable pictures and send postcards to our family and friends back home. Our journey would be just as exciting as our final destination.

The great road trip for our software journey was treated the same way. I used postcards with pictures to send to the staff. Brief, fun notes are telling people what we discovered and identified what we will take with us on our trip. We talked about the detours that we had to take when the path was unexpectedly blocked. And we created a fun and exciting adventure that others wanted to participate. Along the way, we created a vision of the future operation of the business. The change effort was a lasting success.

Pay attention to the culture of the organization when addressing changes. By understanding the behavioral norms and expectations, a change management practitioner can introduce change in a way that is not threatening and can still be very effective. Once the employees understood the change, they were more willing to discover how the software and related process changes could enhance their productivity.

34

GUIDING PRINCIPLES FOR
TRANSFORMATION

*"Some people live an entire lifetime wondering if they've made
a difference in the world, Marines don't have that problem."*

— PRESIDENT RONALD REGAN

ONE OF THE strategic activities within the People and Organization track that I discuss in my book, Business Cards: Transforming the Organization One Card at a Time, is Guiding Principles. The leader of the change initiative will need to have clear in their mind the values, beliefs, and ethical standards in the way they lead and manage the initiative. Defining these guiding principles is important to run a successful transformation initiative. If you don't define your beliefs and values, others will do it for you.

The guiding principles not only will set the tone for the project but will establish the standards in which the members should expect to act. You may ask why this is important. After all, as employees we would expect to have certain values and principles already. In many cases, this is true; we do have certain expectations that have been defined within the organization in which we work. However, a transformational change initiative is different, it is not business as usual. The project requires members to think in new and unique ways. Our competencies will certainly be tested along with our problem-solving and decision-making abilities.

Therefore, it is the leader who needs to define and practice these principles to ensure the initiative follows these standards to ensure a successful mission. We can turn to the U.S. Marine Corps in a time-tested, a proven approach. The Marines have developed guiding principles for their leaders over the past 200+ years. Based on their success, I think they got it right.

1. **Know yourself and seek self-improvement.** No matter how much leaders achieve, there is always room for improvement. One can never have too much knowledge or too many skills. Business leaders should try to live a lifestyle of continual growth.

2. **Develop a sense of responsibility among your employees.** No one can be everywhere all the time. By developing responsibilities among employees throughout the entire organization, an individual doesn't have to be. The business leaders should empower their employees to make decisions and hold them accountable.

3. **Be technically and tactically proficient.** All employees should be trained thoroughly in the mechanics of their job and rigorously tested at least annually in basic skills of their profession. This includes their ability to problem-solve and make informed decisions.

4. **Make sound and timely decisions.** To be effective, business leaders should couple decisiveness with judgment. Know your employees and look out for their welfare. The Marine Corps understands that people are its most valuable resource and so should business leaders. By knowing whom best to delegate tasks to, leaders are then able to accomplish their missions efficiently.

5. **Keep Your Employees Informed.** "Ours is not to reason why, ours is but to do and die." This popular maxim repeated in a scene in

Saving Private Ryan perpetuates the idea that Marines blindly follow orders. While it is true that time does not allow for an explanation in all instances when the time is available, Marines are told the "why" behind the orders. Business leaders must ensure that their employees understand the goals of the organization as well as how they fit into the overall scheme. Leaders need to talk to their employees often, even if it's just to say that everything is going according to plan.

6. **Seek responsibility and take responsibility for your actions.** By taking on responsibility, leaders show that they have confidence in their own abilities. Likewise, when leaders make mistakes, they are encouraged to own up to it. Admitting to their mistakes shows integrity and maturity.

7. **Ensure assigned tasks are understood, supervised and accomplished.** Leaders should be very specific about exactly want they want to be done and who will be responsible for its completion. Strong leaders set deadlines or benchmarks, and they follow up. By being very specific about what needs to be accomplished, the "how" of the task should get pushed as far down the chain of command as possible: this allows for a great deal of flexibility at the smallest group level.

8. **Train your employees as a team.** If an organization has the best employees in the world, it will be meaningless if they don't work together in a coordinated fashion. Make sure that the lines of communication are open among departments. Time should be spent cross-training work groups so that each unit has an understanding of the other unit's responsibilities.

9. **These objectives, principles, and traits are built around simple truths** about human nature and the uncertainties of dynamic work environments. Obviously, these are factors that can have a great impact on any organization. The difference is that the Marines have staked their life on them, which is a strong motivation for getting it right.

Transformational change needs to be a top-down driven approach to be successful. This does not mean that subordinates do not, or should not be empowered to take specific actions to support and align the change vision in their day-to-day activities. By following these guiding principles and those like them, employees will be prepared for any change that comes their way.

35

LEADERSHIP IN THE FACE OF CHANGE

"LEADERSHIP IS THE sum of those qualities of intellect, human understanding, and moral character that enables a person to inspire and control a group of people successfully." This quote from Lieutenant General John A Lejeune of the U.S. Marine Corps eloquently summarized the characteristics of leadership. I used this quote because, over the past 237 years since the founding of the U.S. Marine Corps, they have been successful in creating leaders and completing their objectives. Whether leading a group on the battlefield, running a small business or being the president of the country, leadership is the single most important characteristic needed for success. Leadership isn't about creating followers; it is, however, about creating leaders of others. We inspire others by creating a vision for change, a clear picture of the future. We control people successfully by providing them with enough information to take the appropriate steps to achieve the vision.

There are three types of leaders. Those who learn from reading, those who learn from observation, and those who still have to touch the electric fence to get the message. There are those who believe that leaders are born and not made. Well, we can say that personality traits and intellectual ability play a part, making it easier for some to interact with others, it does not mean that there are born leaders. Like any other skill, one needs to understand the characteristics of leadership and work to develop those skills. General Lejeune was said to be a quiet and unassuming man. Not a man that one would assume would be capable of creating a legend or ever contribute to one. Lejeune none the less created a vision that continues to this day; the vision was the landing from ships of the men and weapons of war to gain a toehold on a hostile shore. This was the vision that became a highly refined mission accredited by the Congress of the United States. The mission is the amphibious attack. However, his vision did not come to fruition in his lifetime. It was his vision, however, that refined strategies and thinking that would evolve into today's modern Marine Corps.

During major change initiatives, there will be a great deal of confusion, speculation, and assumptions about the reasons for the change. It takes a strong leader to guide the team toward your vision. They can only do this if you describe what you believe can get accomplished. This must be more than just a memo, a motivational speech, or a directive. Effective leaders frequently talk about the vision and help others to see the potential. They not only motivate and inspire others but provide them with valuable information that supports their cause.

Effective leaders lead by example; they show others through their actions. They remove barriers that prevent others to achieving the goal. When others believe in what you believe, then the chances are good that the change can be achieved. Now get to work and make change happen.

36

DOING BAD THINGS FASTER

"We cannot make good news out of bad practice."

— EDWARD R. MURROW

THE DIRECTOR OF the I.T. department was tasked to lead an initiative to implement a CRM system across the enterprise, replacing their existing legacy systems. The company was a $6 billion dollar property and casualty company that provided insurance products throughout the United States. It operated five main offices across the country with multiple field offices. Much of their growth was attributed to acquisitions that occurred six years prior to the project. At that time, an effort was made to transition customer records to the existing platform but leave the marketing database residing at the local offices until such time the records could be consolidated into an enterprise-wide CRM application. A solid business case was created showing the benefits of a global view of former, current, and potential customers for improved marketability. A tremendous cost savings could be realized by not having to license and support applications at each office. Overall, the enterprise-wide

CRM system just made sense, and the business case was unanimously approved. The I.T. director formed a selection committee to evaluate the wide assortment of CRM systems currently on the market. After reviewing features and functionality of several systems that were demonstrated, the team made their selection. A budget of $15.5 million dollars was established, and a consulting company was selected to implement the new application.

Within a short time, the project team was established consisting of consultants and selected employees from various parts of the organization. The project team received a great deal of support from senior leadership, and it was apparent that everyone was very supportive and excited about the possibility of the improved visibility to the customer base. Business requirements were gathered and aligned with the capabilities of the software application. A conference room pilot was used to demonstrate the capabilities of the system further building support across the organization. Configuration and testing followed over the following months. Although there were a few unexpected glitches, the problems were quickly resolved, and the live data was converted into the new application. A small team traveled to each office to test and validate the operation of the system. Staff members at each office were trained on the new capabilities to enhance their business operation. When the project was completed, every office had access to the new CRM application, with their data converted, and the staff well trained ready to become more efficient in their work.

An increase in performance and efficiency was not meant to be. Shortly after the last office was trained, employees started to complain about the customer information. Upon closer examination, it turned out that there were multiple records for the same customer. Many customer records showed multiple addresses, telephone numbers, and even multiple spellings of the customer's name. In the project teams haste to configure the application, they failed to look at the data. Although the application with its automated workflow and ease of access made it quicker to access and process information, they failed to do their due diligence to the accuracy of the data. Combining old, outdated or even wrong information with new information from multiple locations crippled this insurance organization from generating new business. It took nearly a year for the organization to recover.

Knowledge is the lifeblood of any organization to not only survive but to maintain a competitive advantage over their competitors. Technology must be thought of as a tool that enables data to be processed, displayed and analyzed in a way that creates knowledge. This is why information and knowledge management are considered a driver of performance. When aligned with the other performance drivers as technology, business processes, and people / organization, true integrated performance can be achieved.

37

BUSINESS VALUES OF PETER BAILY

*"The more moral the people are in their business dealings, the
less paperwork you need, the more handshakes you can have, the
more the wheels of capitalism work better because there's trust
in the marketplace. Business ethics is not a joke. And, in fact, I
think most businesses that I've dealt with encourage exactly that
type of behavior."*

— RICK SANTORUM

ON CHRISTMAS EVE as my family and I await the anticipation of what
tomorrow will bring. The joy of our family being together is a comfort
to all of us as it has been for many years. The Christmas tree is decorated with
bright lights and ornaments that my children have made along with those that
have been passed down to us from years ago.

We have a tradition to open some presents in the evening before heading
off to celebrate Christmas at our parent's home since their age has made it difficult for them to leave their home. These are traditions that have been passed

down from my father. One of those traditions that we did was to watch Frank Capra's 1946 movie, "It's a Wonderful Life". This old movie is about an angel who helps a compassionate but despairingly frustrated businessman by showing what life would have been like if he never existed.

While continuing the tradition this year, there was a line that George Bailey (James Stewart) said that seemed to have real meaning for me in my quest to manage change. Allow me to quote a line from that movie:

"Just a minute... just a minute. Now, hold on, Mr. Potter. You're right when you say my father was no businessman. I know that. Why he ever started this cheap, penny-ante Building and Loan, I'll never know. But neither you nor anyone else can say anything against his character, because his whole life was... why, in the 25 years since he and his brother, Uncle Billy, started this thing, he never once thought of himself. Isn't that right, Uncle Billy? He didn't save enough money to send Harry away to college, let alone me. But he did help a few people get out of your slums, Mr. Potter, and what's wrong with that? Why... here, you're all businessmen here. Doesn't it make them better citizens? Doesn't it make them better customers? You... you said... what'd you say a minute ago? They had to wait and save their money before they even ought to think of a decent home. Wait? Wait for what? Until their children grow up and leave them? Until they're so old and broken down that they... Do you know how long it takes a working man to save $5,000? Just remember this, Mr. Potter that this rabble you're talking about... they do most of the working and paying and living and dying in this community. Well, is it too much to have them work and pay and live and die in a couple of decent rooms and a bath? Anyway, my father didn't think so. People were human beings to him. But to you, a warped, frustrated old man, they're cattle. Well in my book, my father died a much richer man than you'll ever be!"

George Baily was not only describing his father's character traits but describes the values and the vision that he had to run his business. George and the others may not have understood the reasons that drove Peter Baily but they

all knew his vision and the core values he instilled in every employee and customer of the Bailey Building and Loan.   How can we as change agents instill
the same vision and values in our initiative?

Bob Welch has a very interesting book entitled:"52 Little Lessons from
It's a Wonderful Life". This is a wonderful book on life lessons that can be
applied to business.

38

MEASURING SUCCESSFUL CHANGE

"My measure of success is whether I'm fulfilling my mission."

— ROBERT KIYOSAKI

"OK, WE WENT through this long and painful change, now we just hope it solves our problem." Those are the words spoken by many directors and vice-presidents upon completion of their major change initiative. Ready, Fire, Aim, this is the approach many project sponsors take. The completion of the project is not the time to figure out what to measure.

The primary reason for this stance is based on trust. The consulting company that was contracted to implement the change stated that this change was best practice, and there was no reason to doubt them. It would take some time before the employees adjust to the changes; after all, there is a learning curve. Some of the changes are readily visible – new reports show consolidated financials; automated workflow improves processing and analytic tools aid in problem-solving. But the question remains, was the change successful, did the initiative solve the business problem?

The terms metrics and measures are tossed about and used interchangeably to determine the extent of the change. Measures are a component of a metric. If we say that there is $1,000 in our checking account, which is a measure of dollars that have been deposited in the bank, it is just a point in time. We may have required a larger sum of money, or collect it the money over a shorter period of time.

Therefore, a metric is a unit of measure compared to another unit of measure. A unit of measure may be a period of time, the number of units, dollars, the number of people, etc. One unit can be plotted on the "X" axis and the other on the "Y" axis. The result can be expressed as a ratio, percentage, or another unit that best explains the result. An example would be the "Training Cost Expense Percent". The formula for this metric is the percentage of operating expenses that are dedicated to training expenses. The measures are the operating and training expenses. Another example is the "Human Capital ROI", this formula is expressed by the pre-tax profit an organization that is generated for each dollar invested in regular employee's pay and benefits after non-human expenses are removed.

Now that we understand the difference between a metric and a measure, we must determine the appropriate metric or metrics to use. It is important to note that only a few metrics should be used since it is difficult to focus on multiple sets of data. I recommend choosing no more than four metrics. As improvements are made, new metrics can be chosen to focus on other areas related to the change initiative.

There are many operational metrics that have been defined but seldom if at all do you see actual organizational change management metrics that can be used during a large-scale change initiative. Below are some Organizational Change Management metrics that I have defined and used in large-scale change initiatives:

Metric	Formula / Definition
Impact Factor	The total percentage of employees directly impacted by the change: Total EE/Total impacted by the change.

Change investment factor	The number of change activities * cost / number of employees impacted by the change.
Rate of change ratio	The number of change initiatives over a given period of time.
Rate of change – velocity	The number of changed activities over a given period of time.
Rate of Change ratio – momentum	The momentum of change in one initiative relative to another.
Rate of Accelerating Returns	The time span between one change event to another event in the same impact area.
Competency Gap Ratio	The difference between the number of competencies in one group over another
Income Factor Ratio	Takes the pre-tax profit an organization generates and attributes this to each regular full-time equivalent (FTE) before and after the change.
Human Capital ROI	The pre-tax profit an organization generates for each dollar invested in regular employee pay and benefits after non-human expenses are removed.
Human Economic Value Added Ratio	Takes the after-tax profit an organization generates and attributes it to each regular employee full-time equivalent (FTE) before and after the change.
Change implementation ratio	The number of approved change activities to the number of change activities implemented.
Change activity sustained	The number of change activities implemented over a given period of time.
Cost / Benefit Ratio	Benefits of change compared with the costs.
Culture Gap Ratio	The size of the culture gap (average three primary indicators) to the time to close the gap to the defined benchmark.

39

MAKING SACRIFICES TO
ACCOMPLISH OUR GOAL?

"Football is like life - it requires perseverance, self-denial, hard work, sacrifice, dedication and respect for authority."

— VINCE LOMBARDI

I RECENTLY WORKED WITH the Vice President of business operations on a globalization initiative for an international bank to ensure that the employees were prepared for the upcoming change that was about to take place.

The bank was implementing new credit card processing software as they transitioned a portion of their services to an outsourcing provider. The bank prided themselves on providing a unique customer experience. Over the years, they had built processes and systems that focused on delivering custom services and products. These were their market differentiators that have positioned them to grow in a depressed economic market.

Both the outsourcing provider and the new software application provided differences that were seen as constraints on the business operation. It was the intent to keep the application as vanilla as possible to reduce costs and avoid issues in future upgrades. As the project progressed, small deviations were identified such as the ability to change interest rates at any point in time to the end of the month. Managers saw this change as seemingly insignificant and not worth the added cost and time to submit a change request, go through the approval process, and assign the resources to make the change.

There appeared to be many similar small changes that had to be reviewed by the business analysts and the functional managers. There was reluctance on the manager's part to approve the change. "This is how we have always done it" was their mantra. Since the managers were directed by the executives to not allow customization of the application, they were uncertain of the potential impact the change would have. The change would also result in an increase in project cost and time delays.

What was not realized was each change moved the organization further away from their core value of providing a unique customer experience? Each small change was a departure from their value proposition. Conforming to the new, generic standard may result in a cost savings of thousands of dollars in the project. However, it is difficult to determine the cost of a decrease in customer satisfaction and loyalty that leads to a decrease in revenue.

Core values are the very significant beliefs and principles that define the business. They are specialized standards set by a company regarding the method of its functioning, decision-making, problem-solving, and customer service. The primary benefit of core values is that they let employees and potential consumers know what the company is all about and clarifies the identity of the company.

Defining core values and aligning them into the change initiative are strategic activities that have been identified in my book, Business Cards: Transforming the Organization One Card at a Time. The core values will establish the framework in which the change can take place and be successful.

The decisions came down to cost cutting measures versus sustaining customer satisfaction. The project became the urgent need that was counter to the prevailing organizational culture supported by the core value of creating an outstanding customer experience. The delays in decision making were managers who resisted deviating from those core values. The project experienced several delays and undoubtedly resulted in a decrease in both employee and customer satisfaction.

40

Changing Minds and Behaviors

"It's better to hang out with people better than you. Pick out associates whose behavior is better than yours, and you'll drift in that direction."

— Warren Buffett

M OST PEOPLE WOULD agree that organizational change management is needed to ensure the success of the project. What most people would not agree on is if it changes the way we think about the change or if it changes the behavior. Some people would argue that change management achieves both through the two main objectives communication and training. The change management tasks in a project plan, for the most part, are focused on identifying the stakeholder groups and delivering key messages regarding the project in a timely fashion without raising stress levels. Later, the attention shifts to developing and delivering training to the stakeholder group to be taught a new skill.

In a previous chapter entitled Is Change Management Worth It? I described the difference between the two different types of change communication: Key messages and Behavioral messaging. In there I stated "**Key Message Communication**" is defined as the delivery of any information that does not require action. Any communication for which there is no discernible consequence if the recipient ignores it. "**Behavioral Communication**" is the delivery of any information, in any form or format, designed to drive a specific action with clearly defined measures, consequences, and rewards." These two types of messaging either informs or requires an action, but does not necessarily change our mind.

Some would, therefore, argue that the information aids in formulating new opinions which in turn will help change our mind and behavior. Let's examine this further. We can communicate using various vehicles such as: verbally using speeches, phone calls, discussion groups, etc. or visual communication using emails, web pages, flyers, etc. Although we have many ways of delivering the messages, how much will our audience actually remember? Short term memory is broken into three distinct parts based on the three different modes: hearing, visual, and chunking.

The hearing mode also called the phonological loop is where we hear sounds but only have the ability to remember about two seconds of sound for up to two minutes depending upon if we repeat the information or not. That is if you are trying to remember a phone number, but someone is distracting you while you are attempting to remember it, the information will fade by about two minutes. If you are able to rehearse it, by repeating it over and over, it can be remembered for longer periods of time.

The visual mode also called the visuospatial sketchpad is where we are able to keep something visualized for recall. We are capable of storing about 1 – 3 images depending upon one's personal ability. Since we are bombarded with many visual images, we can only remember the details of the image for about 30 seconds.

The chunking mode is the ability to group information into easier storage in short term memory and will greatly improve the phonological loop's capacity. However, you can only chunk so much information at one time and still be useful. There is a limit of how many chunks of information that you can store at once. People usually forget the middle portions of information. Remembering the beginning and ending is called the primacy and recency effect.

Although change communication is critically important, it needs to be used to reinforce other change management activities. It does, however, reinforce the need to communicate frequently using a variety of vehicles.

When we think of training, we think of adherence, testing, drills, exercises, and standards. When we are formally trained, we are being groomed to perform tasks, according to a set of expectations. Training focuses on the acquisition of new skills whereas learning focuses on achieving permanent changes in behavior. Learning uses cognitive abilities, acquired knowledge and experience to formulate new experiences. It requires trial and error over a longer period of time.

During a project, we may train employees what to do to use the new software application but make the assumption that employees know why they are performing those actions. Therefore, if something out of the ordinary occurs, their actions are heavily influenced by the current culture that exists that influences their behavior and, therefore, will revert to their old ways.

In order to change minds and behaviors, change management must look beyond the traditional communication and training activities and focus on those things that influence behavior (culture) and create a learning environment that reinforces the new behavior.

41

PITFALLS OF REQUIREMENTS GATHERING

*"The most difficult part of requirements gathering is not the act
of recording what the user wants; it is the exploratory development activity of helping users figure out what they want."*

— STEVE McCTONNELL

INADEQUATELY DEFINED REQUIREMENTS have been one of the biggest reasons that projects fall behind schedule, go over budget, and fail to meet
the expectations of the project. One of the first activities within a project is
to gather requirements. The task of requirements gathering is usually delegated to the business analyst who identifies stakeholders to question. The
process of gathering requirements is straightforward. The business analyst
will identify all of the stakeholders who are determined to be impacted by the
change. Then, the Business Analyst will interview each stakeholder to identify each task, and document in detail how the stakeholder performs that task.
During that process, the Business Analyst will identify any tools that may be
used to perform the task, such as a calculator, a spreadsheet, or some other

device or application. In addition, any policies or regulatory requirements that govern the performance of the tasks are documented. Being careful to capture each statement accurately, the Business Analyst creates the requirements document. Once complete, the requirements document is reviewed with the stakeholder to ensure that it precisely reflects the task as described by the stakeholder. Once the requirements document has been approved by the stakeholder, it is then submitted to the project manager for distribution, completing the assignment.

Although this is the typical approach used to collect requirements for a project, there are inherent flaws in this approach. I have identified four key assumptions and their ramifications to the success of a transformation initiative.

Assumption 1: Stakeholders know how to perform the job tasks correctly.

Stakeholders may not have received the same training. Some employees learn on the job without the aid of guides and manuals. Bad habits, shortcuts, or simply not being aware of an acceptable standard may create a potential risk.

Assumption 2: Other stakeholders may disagree that the tasks were reported correctly.

Not all stakeholders who have similar job roles perform tasks the same way. The process of performing a task may vary from one department to the next depending upon their unique guidelines and conditions. What is acceptable in one area may be rejected in another.

Assumption 3: All of the job tasks have been captured.

Most stakeholders are very familiar with performing routine tasks; however exceptions or tasks that need to be performed randomly, quarterly, yearly or during unique situations may be overlooked or documented incorrectly.

ASSUMPTION 4: THE REQUIREMENTS WILL BE
THE SAME AFTER THE TRANSFORMATION.

The most critical of all of the assumptions is that the requirements are being captured under current conditions rather than future state conditions. How the task is performed may radically change or may even be eliminated based on how the future state process is designed.

Based on these assumptions the likelihood that the requirements that were collected are complete, accurate and reflect the needs of the future state design are greatly diminished and, therefore, can place the project at greater odds of failure.

To increase the success factor, I have used collaborative workshops to document the current and future state requirements through process mapping. Creating an end-to-end process flow map of the current state can identify such things as input and output requirements, activities and tasks, key decision points, hand-off points to other areas, policies and business rules, as well as tools and systems used. Process disconnects, bottlenecks, and inefficiencies are easily identified.

In the process of creating the future state, the group examines industry best practices and new capabilities that can be achieved. A gap analysis is performed, and a list of new requirements can be created. During this collaborative process, all stakeholders are involved in documentation and understanding the nuances. Upon completion, stakeholders not only are in agreement but have been an active participant in the design which leads greater acceptance to the change.

42

WHAT'S YOUR MOBILE STRATEGY?

"There is always a better strategy than the one you have; you just haven't thought of it yet."

— SIR BRIAN PITMAN

LET'S FACE IT; we live in an age of instant gratification. When we want to communicate with someone, find out a sports score, deposit a check into our bank account or purchase a movie ticket, we turn to our mobile phone or tablet. Within seconds, we tweeted a friend, conducted our business, and now spend some time searching the net.

The technology and capabilities have advanced for individuals and businesses to go mobile. In fact, research shows that more than 20 percent of the total online traffic is now mobile. Projections suggest that 72 percent of the world's population will be mobile by the year 2016!

The most important technology product no longer sits on your desk but rather fits in your hand. Mobile phones and tablets have become the most prevalent tool for media consumption and communication worldwide. There are 4.6 billion mobile phone subscriptions are now in use. Compare that to the 1.2 billion personal computers that are currently in use (including laptops), that number is staggering. Eighty-three percent of American adults own a mobile phone, and this number is even higher for American adults ages 18-29 (93%). Tablet ownership, in general, has skyrocketed in recent years; just 3 percent of adults owned one in May 2010, but that number rose to 25 percent by August 2012 and then to 34 percent in May of 2013.

However, with that amount of usage, business leaders are still struggling to figure out how to connect to their customers. Marketers tend to focus on building mobile applications, web design and placement of QR codes -- the functional level details at which these are used. Leveraging these technical trends is not a mobile strategy. These activities can be costly and divert attention away from the intended purpose of the mobile strategy, which is to connect customers and potential customers to the business to satisfy their needs.

The information from social media sites such as Facebook, Twitter, and other sources should connect to the company's CRM system to build a customer profile of their needs, concerns, and desires. The mobile strategy is more about the behaviors and attitudes of the customer than it is about the technology used to connect with that person. A well-defined business case is needed to define the metrics and measures for success.

The development of a mobile strategy should not be an isolated event; rather, it must be placed into the context of a transformational change initiative. The mobile technical solution influences or is influenced by the organization's technical architectural principles, as well as business continuity and disaster recovery at the strategic level, by determining how information is accessed, distributed, and controlled. In addition, the mobile technical solution is influenced by the people and organizational systems, defined business processes, and the management of information and knowledge. Alignment must occur across the people, process, technology, and information performance tracks to ensure it is properly positioned to be successful within the organization.

Allow me to illustrate my point. There may be a strong desire to utilize mobile devices, place information in the cloud, and to leverage social networking to allow the business to be more flexible and respond to their customer base. The concept or even the technology may be viewed as too risky in its delivery, operation or perceived quality. Who within the organization would be permitted to communicate with the public from Twitter, Facebook, or other social sites? Are their business policies that need to be changed or does it violate some regulatory compliance law? And, will the prevailing culture of the organization trust employees with the mobile freedom and exchange of information that this mobile technology has to offer? These are strategic questions that need to be addressed during the transformational planning phase of the initiative. Once addressed, then a different set of questions and alignment issues arise from the tactical, operational, and functional levels of the initiative that must be addressed.

With the technical systems configured, the information managed, the business processes redefined, and the organization that is aligned with a culture that will embrace the change, then and only then can the mobile capabilities be successful.

43

CORPS LEADERSHIP

"You cannot allow any of your people to avoid the brutal facts.
If they start living in a dream world, it's going to be bad."

— GENERAL JAMES 'MAD DOG' MATTIS

WHETHER YOU ARE the boss of a small business or the President of the United States, it is essential to be a strong and well-defined leader to guide people to do their best. Leadership requires clearly defined objectives, traits, and principles to be effective and to create lasting success.

Fred Smith, the founder of the highly successful FedEx Corporation, stated in the Legacy newsletter that he acknowledged that the United States Marine Corps played a vital role in shaping his life. He also noted the business achievements of other Marines in the corporate world. Smith was quoted in the article saying, "Nothing has prepared business leaders better for their roles in business and society than the lessons they learned in the Corps — lessons of discipline, organization, commitment, and integrity." Everything about the

Marines — their culture, their organizational structure, their management style and their decision-making process — is geared toward creating a high-speed, high-complexity environment. This situation is similar to those elements found in large-scale change initiatives within organizations.

There are three fundamental categories that every U.S. Marine is instructed in leadership objectives, leadership traits, and leadership principles. Business leaders would benefit from learning and applying these lessons to their organization.

There are two leadership objectives. The primary objective of Marine Corps leadership is mission accomplishment. This requires a goal-oriented approach. A leader must identify long-term goals for the team and the short-term steps the organization needs to take to achieve those goals. The secondary objective of leadership is troop (employee) welfare —also described as team welfare or individual welfare. This objective requires empathy on the part of the leader to make sure that the needs of those in the team are looked after.

There are fourteen traits to which all Marines are encouraged to aspire. They are judgment, justice, dependability, integrity, decisiveness, tact, initiative, enthusiasm, bearing, unselfishness, courage, knowledge, loyalty and endurance. Marines are encouraged to exhibit these traits and are judged on their ability to do so. When these leadership traits are applied to business, they aid in the development of a strong, adaptive and constructive culture that encourages all employees to do their best.

Marines are encouraged to memorize and are often required to recite the fourteen leadership traits at inspections, but it is not required for them to memorize the definitions. The Marine Corps would rather its marines contemplate what they mean for themselves. One might assume the Marine Corps does this to ensure individuals internalize these traits by coming up with their own definitions. The same is true about attaching priorities to these traits. For instance, is "judgment" a more important trait than "decisiveness"? The Marine Corps leadership system doesn't specify, unlike the leadership objectives which are described in terms of "primary" and "secondary."

The last component of the Marine Corps leadership system is the set of Marine Corps leadership principles. As the objectives and traits, these principles are given to the Marines to set goals for their attitudes and behaviors. I will state these leadership principles in business terms:

Know yourself and seek self-improvement. No matter how much leaders achieve, there is always room for improvement. One can never have too much knowledge or too many skills. Business leaders should try to live a lifestyle of continual growth.

Develop a sense of responsibility among your employees. No one can be everywhere all the time. By developing responsibility among employees throughout the entire organization, an individual doesn't have to be. The business leaders should empower their employees to make decisions and hold them accountable.

Be technically and tactically proficient. All employees should be trained thoroughly in the mechanics of their job and rigorously tested at least annually in basic skills of their profession. This includes their ability to problem-solve and make informed decisions.

Make sound and timely decisions. To be effective, business leaders should couple decisiveness with judgment. Know your employees and look out for their welfare. The Marine Corps understands that people are its most valuable resource and so should business leaders. By knowing whom best to delegate tasks to, leaders are then able to accomplish their missions efficiently.

Keep Your Employees Informed. "Ours is not to reason why, ours is but to do and die." This popular maxim repeated in a scene in *Saving Private Ryan* perpetuates the idea that Marines blindly follow orders. While it is true that time does not allow for an explanation in all instances when the time is available, Marines are told the "why" behind the orders. Business leaders must ensure that their employees understand the goals of the organization as well as how they fit into the overall scheme. Leaders need to talk to their employees often, even if it's just to say that everything is going according to plan.

Seek responsibility and take responsibility for your actions. By taking on responsibility, leaders show that they have confidence in their own abilities. Likewise, when leaders make mistakes, they are encouraged to own up to it. Admitting to their mistakes shows integrity and maturity.

Ensure assigned tasks are understood, supervised and accomplished. Leaders should be very specific about exactly what tasks they want to be completed and who will be responsible for its completion. Strong leaders set deadlines or benchmarks, and they follow up. By being very specific about what needs to be accomplished, the "how" of the task should get pushed as far down the chain of command as possible? This allows for a great deal of flexibility at the smallest group level.

Train your employees as a team. If an organization has the best employees in the world, it will be meaningless if they don't work together in a coordinated fashion. Make sure that the lines of communication are open among departments. Time should be spent cross-training work groups so that each unit has an understanding of the other unit's responsibilities.

These objectives, principles, and traits are built around simple truths about human nature and the uncertainties of dynamic work environments. Obviously, these are factors that can have a great impact on any organization. The difference is that the Marines have based their life on them, which is a strong motivation for getting it right.

44

TRANSFORMATION – WHAT
DOES IT REALLY MEAN?

*"An organization's ability to learn, and translate that learning
into action rapidly is the ultimate competitive advantage."*

— JACK WELCH

RAFAEL, A SENIOR comptroller, was meeting with an account executive
from a large consulting firm discussing issues in the company's accounting software. With the rapid growth of the company over the past couple of
years, it had become increasingly difficult to manage the finances effectively.
Rafael explained that some departments were using spreadsheets for budgeting, tracking lot numbers of products, and to audit inventory. Although we
found ways in with to work around some of these issues, Rafael told the account executive, there were other areas that they could not resolve such as
reporting.

It was clear to the account executive that their current accounting software package no longer met the needs of this rapidly growing company. What would you say if I was able to provide a software application that would streamline your budgeting process, track lot, and serial numbers, manage inventory and provide dashboards allowing departmental managers to make informed decisions? Eager to resolve these issues, Rafael asked the account executive to provide a proposal and set up a demonstration.

Returning a few days later, the account executive was armed with a PowerPoint deck and his laptop to demonstrate the new software. Present at the meeting was the CFO, a couple of department managers, the head of I.T., and Rafael. The account executive promoted the software as transforming the organization through integration, automation, and enhanced reporting. The demonstration provided a generic overview of some common transactional processing in accounts payable, accounts receivable, purchase orders, and budgeting. Impressed with the demonstration and software capabilities, they signed on to the transformation project. But what is transformative about this project?

Transformation, by definition, is the process of profound and radical change that orients an organization in a new direction and takes it to an entirely different level of effectiveness. One could argue that a new enterprise software application creates a transformation due to its inherent capabilities to integrate transactional processes, automate administrative tasks and provide collaboration between functional areas and departments. These changes are neither at the strategic, tactical or operational, level, but rather impact work performed at the functional level. This is the area where specific individuals perform work tasks. Although there can be noticeable improvements in efficiency, it is by no means "Transformational".

The new software application is a tool to enable tasks to be performed across the organization in a standardized way, much like a nail gun provides greater efficiency over a hammer, but it doesn't build the house better.

So, do we limit the transformation as a "radical" departure from the way the business operates? Transformation should focus on answering the core business problem rather than the symptoms. A core business problem may be, for example, improving customer support and loyalty; creating competitive advantage through innovation and adapting quickly to change. To solve these business problems and achieve these goals requires an integrated approach.

An integrated and aligned approach orientates the organization in a new direction to resolve the stated problem. The transformation re-positions the way in which the organization operates along four lines: people and organization; business processes; technology; and information and knowledge management. The organizational culture or the common behaviors will need to support the core values of the organization providing a collaborative work environment. The organization may need to redefine job roles and reporting relationships. After all, if the technology automates many of the manual tasks, what will employees do with the extra time? Non-value added tasks should be eliminated from business processes, and critical processes need to be standardized. New technology should be selected to enhance the business process not define it. Information should be placed in the hands of employees who need it to problem-solve effectively and make informed decisions. Knowledge should be captured and shared to eliminate redundant mistakes and to grow the organization based upon lessons learned.

So, business transformation is not technology, nor is it a large, complex project. Transformation is making a change in the way in which the business currently operates to eliminate or avoid a problem that places the organization at risk. Transformation activities start with a clear vision for change and ensure that all of the current capabilities are aligned to support the change. Transformation activities are integrated and have a cause-and-effect relationship. Transformation activities must start at a strategic level and driven down to the functional detailed tasks. For example: if the change vision is to improve customer satisfaction, than the functional tasks may be changing work steps to make it easier for the customer and employee, rewarding good behavior, getting the right information to the employee at the right time, in the right format to allow them to make informed decisions.

45

REWARDING CONSTRUCTIVE BEHAVIOR

"The most difficult thing is the decision to act; the rest is merely tenacity. The fears are paper tigers. You can do anything you decide to do. You can act to change and control your life, and the procedure, the process is its own reward."

— AMELIA EARHART

EVERY EMPLOYEE HAS a need to be recognized and acknowledged by those they work with on a day-to-day basis, including managers and peers for their work contribution. Recognition is essentially positive feedback that lets employees know they are valued and appreciated by their co-workers and the organization. To have the greatest impact in the workplace, recognition activities should also reinforce and encourage work that advances employee, departmental, and institutional goals and values. Recognition is one of the basic human needs that will acknowledge that they belong to a group. To a certain degree, the act of recognition maintains self-esteem, respect, or a sense of worth.

Employee recognition is fundamentally about relationships. The behaviors and expectations of a person align and are accepted by the larger group. As a result, their common behavior will continue to be supported and encouraged. There are times when people sense there is not a good "fit" for the individual employee. That person may appear to be different through subtle actions, or conversations. The biases are brought about by the prevailing organizational culture that may be strong enough to force the employee to either comply or leave.

During a large-scale change where the business is being transformed, the thoughts, beliefs, and expectations are challenged. What once was acceptable behavior can no longer be tolerated. Skipping work steps, making exceptions to the rules, or by-passing approvals may have been encouraged to get the job done on time are examples of acceptable practices supported by the current culture. These are activities that employees were being recognized and rewarded for their initiative. Now, performing these same actions are punishable offenses. Employees can become confused, and their level of stress will rise. As a natural reaction to the change, employees will resist leaving their comfort zone. Without first clearly defining the vision for change employees will continue to push back and do things to block the changes.

The vision for change should describe what the organization will look and how it will operate in the future. Change vision communication should describe at a level of detail how employee's jobs will change in terms of knowledge, skills, and abilities, leaving no doubt as to what an employee should expect. A successful transformative initiative should be aligned with the organization's core values. The change vision, therefore, reflects the desired behaviors, thoughts, and expectations that describe how technical systems, business process, and the reporting structure will be defined and built.

As the initiative moves forward, short-term wins are defined establishing goals. Employees who participate in achieving these goals are recognized for their effort. Public recognition by their managers and in front of their peers provides a powerful example of the new behaviors that were followed. Those employees who continued to follow old, undesirable behaviors should not get punished, but their recognition and reward incentive removed.

Communication around achieving the short term win should describe the new behavior as well as the outcome that was achieved. When employees can tie their actions to results in measurable terms, then and only then can they relate to the value it provides. The employee should be able to connect the single behavior directly to the organization's core value and strategic goal.

Rewarding new behaviors should be commensurate with the amount and degree of effort. Recognition is a big part of the reward. However, each generation has differing reward requirements. Although it is important to reward the individual employee for the desired behaviors, it is also important to promote the team and the organization. Recognizing and rewarding individual performance fails to promote a strong collaborative and constructive culture. Therefore, the criteria should reflect what that individual did in providing value to the organization to support the mission and strategic goals.

Constructive behavior is fostered when everyone within the organization is aligned to the same vision, defined by the core values and is recognized and supported by their contribution. A constructive culture is formed when individuals routinely behave the same supportive way and have the same values and expectations that balance achievement, collaboration, and team synergies. Recognizing and rewarding individuals that align with the goals of the organization will create a synergy and, therefore, strengthen the constructive culture.

46

CLARIFYING BEST PRACTICES

*"Innovation and best practices can be sown throughout an orga-
nization - but only when they fall on fertile ground."*

— MARCUS BUCKINGHAM

BUSINESS BEST PRACTICES are proven, repeatable, documented techniques
that deliver measurable business performance improvements. Executives
look at business best practice benchmarks to help them speed their progress
toward enterprise performance management improvement and to guide them
around pitfalls that might otherwise slow or even halt their initiatives

A best practice is a method or technique that has consistently shown results
superior to those achieved by other means, and that is used as a benchmark.
In addition, a "best" practice can evolve to become better as improvements are
discovered. Some consider Best practices as a business buzzword, used to describe the process of developing and following a standard way of doing things
that multiple organizations can use.

Some consulting firms specialize in the area of Best Practice and offer pre-made 'templates' to standardize business process documentation. Sometimes a "best practice" is not applicable or is inappropriate for a particular organization's needs. A key strategic talent required when applying best practice to organizations is the ability to balance the unique qualities of an organization with the practices that it has in common with others.

Best Practices Defined:

- Aligns with strategy
- Reduces costs
- Improves productivity
- Promotes timely execution
- Enable better decision-making
- Leverages and exploits existing and emerging technologies
- Ensures acceptable levels of control and risk management
- Optimizes the skills and capabilities of the organization
- Promotes collaboration across the extended enterprise

The Levels of Best Practices:

Proven Best Practices: Sustainable and repeatable practices that have been found to be both effective and efficient are considered to be best practices. An effective practice produces consistently satisfactory results to accomplish the purpose which produces the intended or the expected result. Efficient practices perform or function in the best possible manner with the least waste of time and effort. There are several key metrics that are used to determine the sustainability and overall value of a practice to earn the title of proven best practice. Some measures that are used include cost, error rates, quality levels, cycle times, and adaptability. Many proven best practices are incorporated into many software applications and promoted as value-added features and functionality.

Key Elements of a Proven Best Practice:

- Sustainable and replaceable results that achieve efficiency and effectiveness standards
- Has an established clearly defined metrics and measures
- The practice can adapt to incremental changes and continue to maintain its performance
- Practices are effective in replicating the same consistent results across different industries
- The practice achieves maximum productivity reliably with minimum wasted effort or expense

Emerging Practice: Beginning with the objective of assessing what has been learned, and then identifying successful practices from those lessons which are worthy of replication. A lesson learned may have negative or positive aspects. An emerging best practice should demonstrate clear potential for substantiating a cause and effect relationship and can also show potential for replicating across multiple settings and or emerge from a simple, technically specific application.

Key Elements of an Emerging Best Practice:

- Results appear to be sustainable trending towards efficiency and effectiveness standards
- Has an established clearly defined metric and measures
- Practices establish a new and consistent, higher set of standards
- The practice appears to achieve maximum productivity reliably with minimum wasted effort or expense

OBSERVED BEST PRACTICE:

Observed best practices often come about through innovation. Disruptive innovation improves a product or service in ways that the market does not expect, typically first by designing for a different set of consumers in the new market and later by lowering prices in the existing market. Sustaining innovation, on the other hand, evolves existing practices with better value, allowing the firms within to compete against each other's sustaining improvements. Sustaining innovations may be either "discontinuous" (i.e. "transformational" or "revolutionary") or "continuous" (i.e. "evolutionary").

Key Elements of an Observed Best Practice:

- New technology and practices make noticeable improvements
- Practices may run counter to traditional or currently accepted ways
- Sustainability of improvement is not proven over a period of time
- Performance may vary depending upon various situations

BEST PRACTICE FIT

Not all best practices fit a particular organization. This is due to a number of factors such as process or technical maturity levels, financial constraints, sequencing of projects, organizational culture, or other factors. Let's assume that a best practice would be to have all payroll checks directly deposited into the employee's bank account. However, the company employs day laborers who may not have a bank account, and may require a paycheck at the end of the day.

One of the most common reasons for pursuing best practices in a given area is to avoid having to "reinvent the wheel." The reality is best practices are disparate groups of methodologies, processes, rules, concepts and theories that attained a level of success in certain areas, and because of those successes, have been deemed as universal truths able to be applied in specific situations. Knowing and applying best practices saves time and money. It should not be a substitute for innovation and adaptability, quality problem-solving and decision-making, customer and employee satisfaction, and quality of service and products.

47

CONTROLLED CHAOS

*"The significant problems we face today cannot be solved at the
same level of thinking we used to create them."*

— ALBERT EINSTEIN

M OST CORPORATE INITIATIVES fail to live up to their full potential. This
fact is supported by many case studies, published research articles, and
infamous stories told throughout organizations. Executives identify strategic
initiatives with the goal of transforming their business to gain efficiencies, reduce operating expenses, and improve quality; yet to achieve these objectives
most often the focus of attention is only in a functional area or the implementation of some type of technology.

As the process unfolds, management's attention becomes focused even
more on the technology – why, because it is relatively safe. It maintains a level
of controllability for the leadership team. Let me describe a typical example.
The business unit manager undoubtedly had an ongoing problem and raised a

lot of noise about it to the right people above to get their attention. This issue was probably a direct result of financial or quality issues that were faced by other business units or those senior. But it didn't stop there. The unit manager also had to have a proposed solution, and what a better way than to seek a technical solution. Heaven knows that there could not be anything wrong with the work process, the competencies of the workforce, or even shall I dare to say the management style. The foregone conclusion is that it has to be the technical systems. Information is then gathered from outside vendors who espouse the features of their products which provide credence to the solution. Who could not benefit from workflow automation or fancy reports? At the right price and the justification in hand, the immediate problem could be resolved and yes, there could be value to other business units as well.

As the initiative moves forward, the risks are minimized, but so are the overall benefits of the transformation effort. In fact, another layer of complexity was added to the business operation. Now the I.T. department must maintain the application by providing user support, install upgrades and patches, build interfaces to other legacy systems and manage license fees. The workforce will have to take time out of their busy schedule to receive training on the new application putting aside the work already in progress on their desks. Although the automated workflow provided efficiencies to control the information, the work processes had to be altered to accommodate the change. In some instances, the work may be duplicated by maintaining hard copies of documents as well as the system generated data. Managers now have the tools to generate reports and analyze the numbers. Embraced by some, tolerated by others, and not used by a few managers, the new reports reveal a new set of issues that were not previously measured.

The cycle will continue resulting in more firefighting problems and battling change. The opportunity for transformational change was missed. Why? Unfortunately, when organizations operate as a stable, equilibrium-seeking system, they accept only the facts and ideas that conform to their current structure. That produces a stalemate in which organizational change becomes increasingly difficult and often occurs only when faced with a crisis.

To do this, it must change the very basis on which the organization operates. It must evaluate its culture (behavioral norms and expectations) along with its maturity level of its business processes, the way knowledge is managed, and the alignment of its technologies.

48

Eliminating Confusion
about Process

*"Almost all quality improvement comes via simplification of
design, manufacturing... layout, processes, and procedures."*

— Tom Peters

Linda, the comptroller for a mid-market eye care clinic, had commissioned a project to implement a new ERP application that would replace their antiquated payroll application. Their current payroll system worked sufficiently for many years, but as the clinic grew, so did their problems. With several new locations across Florida, Georgia, and South Carolina, the payroll manager found it increasingly difficult to manage multiple state and local taxes. In addition, managing employee benefits was a labor intensive job. Employer and employee contributions to health and life insurance had to be downloaded to a spreadsheet from other applications, manipulated then uploaded into the payroll application. The comptroller also found it difficult to report expenses by location. Something had to change, and a new ERP system was the answer.

The decision was made to manage the project internally, using their own staff they felt their internal knowledge of the business and technical systems would save money and time. However, a functional consultant was needed who had knowledge of the new application and would lead the configuration effort. The project team was established comprising of a business analyst, functional lead, and a database administrator. The three consultants, each with their mission, set off to gather requirements for their perspective areas.

The business analyst needed to understand how the clinic managed their business process from end-to-end. This started with a time card entry all the way through to posting the transaction into the general ledger. As the business analyst gathered the requirements, she talked to the payroll manager and other people about the activities and tasks they perform in the process.

The functional lead needed to configure the application the way the clinic performed their payroll process by configuring the screens. In order to do so, he needed to understand which modules to implement within the ERP system to make the process flow seamlessly.

The database administrator needed to identify and manage the process of data from multiple sources so it can feed into the new ERP system. In his requirements, the DBA talked about the process of moving data from various databases and creating interfaces.

As the requirements gathering phase continued, the payroll manager was concerned about changes in their current procedures brought about by the new functionality of the ERP system. The payroll manager needed to define the new work steps that would be needed to process payroll.

It soon became apparent that the project team and the stakeholders were getting quite confused as the requirement process continued. The confusion came from one word that everyone used differently; the word was "Process". As a result, the requirements were not being communicated clearly and had the potential to cause the new ERP system not to function as desired.

Each person on the team had a different understanding of what process meant to them. With their own point of reference, they would use the word "Process" assuming that the other person knew what they were talking about.

The Payroll Manager referred to "Process" as the work steps needed to run a payroll cycle. She was concerned about each specific task and how it would be different. The Functional lead referred to "Process" as the transactional tasks and how they needed to be configured within the modules of the software application. The Database Administrator referred to "Process" as how data flowed between the database and the applications. And the Business Analyst referred to "Process" as a set of related activities that defined payroll processing. With these diverse frames of reference among the different roles, the ability to define the requirements were compromised.

Without a clear understanding of the business requirements and the future state needs, the project was destined to fail. Their concerns led to a meeting where the questions were listed:

1. Where are all of the places where this new ERP application would change the business process?
2. What policies and regulations would dictate the implementation and the business process?
3. What are the major activities that are performed when processing payroll?
4. What are the tasks to process payroll and who performs them?
5. What are the critical decisions that needed to be made, and who will make those decisions?
6. What other systems and processes are impacted by the change?
7. What information is required to process, report, and monitor?
8. What are the new procedures and work steps?
9. Who needs to be trained?
10. What are the new quality and performance standards?

All of these questions are part of the business process and must be understood and accepted before the project can proceed. First, I will define the business process, and then describe how it should be viewed to capture the right information.

A business process is defined as a set of related activities and tasks that have a defined input or inputs, and a defined output that provides value to the customer. The best way to illustrate a "process" is to describe it in levels. The diagram below illustrates the four process levels.

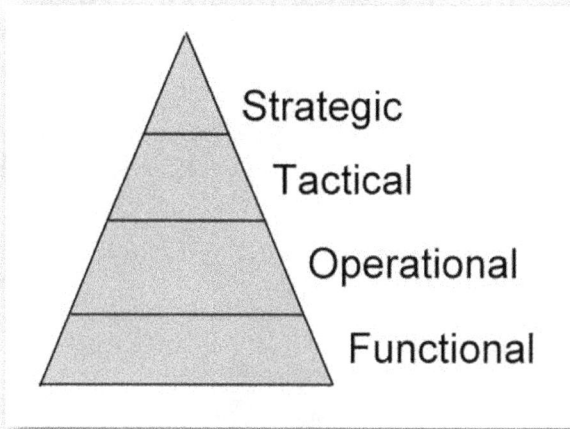

The strategic level: Maps the value chain of the business operation. It defines the activities that are performed for each link that creates value. Measurable outcomes are defined and measured for each link in the value chain. Policies and high-level business rules can be defined that this level.

The Tactical Level: Examines the related sub-processes within the identified function. In our example, this would identify the activities such as payroll administration including time reporting and benefits administration within the human capital management process.

The Operational Level: Defines the activities and tasks along with key decision points, hand-offs to other areas, and systems that are used in performing these tasks. Mapping these tasks are performed within swim lanes that identify job roles and systems that control specific activities.

The Functional Level: Describes the specific procedures in performing a task. Procedures include work steps along with quality and performance standards.

A Business Process (Strategic) is comprised of two or more related Sub-Processes (Tactical) which are defined similar to the business process with the exception that it has a supporting role in the higher-level process. A

Sub-Process is comprised of a group of related Activities (Operational). An Activity is comprised of a group of related Tasks (Functional). Tasks can be broken down into procedures or work steps.

It is essential to the success of the project that each level is identified and addressed to ensure that all of the requirements have been gathered and that everyone has a common understanding of the process and is in agreement.

49

MANAGING PERCEPTIONS
TO ENABLE CHANGE

*"Perception is strong and sight weak. In strategy, it is important
to see distant things as if they were close and to take a distanced
view of close things."*

— AUTHOR UNKNOWN

WHERE DOES THE real value come from in a large-scale change initiative and why is this important to the change management practitioner? First we must identify and understand the perspective in which a person or group of people see the value. Second, we must be able to combine these different perspectives to create a logical understanding of the value. Then we, as change management practitioners must be able to chunk the value into milestones. These three steps are critical to managing the perceptions of the various stakeholders and to affirm the satisfaction they will achieve through the change initiative.

In an organization undergoing change, there are various groups of people performing various roles. Each of these individuals within the group not only have their own values and beliefs, but he or she are influenced by their environment. Those individuals who work in engineering or technical areas use their own standard methodologies and approaches that use logic to derive the technical solution. Other individuals who work in financial areas use their methodologies and approaches to derive a logical economic solution. Many large-scale change initiatives historically have been based on a combination of both a technical and economic solution. Using a cost / benefit analysis, the solution was derived from this logic. However, logic is not its own answer. Just because the solution is faster or cheaper does not make it better. There is another type of solution that is equally important that focuses on emotion rather than logic. These psychological solutions are based upon what individuals' value and believe. In conversation, you may hear people say that they know that logically a solution makes sense but it just doesn't "feel right", or that they have a "gut feeling" about the success of the solution.

I have described the three individual perspectives: financial, technical, and behavioral. But we as good employees were expected to have some sort of behavioral change based on the rationale of logic from the technical and economic solution. To enable change and achieve our desired goal, there must be a blending of all three perspectives.

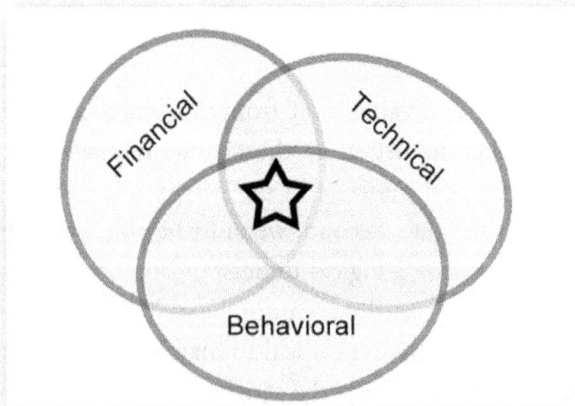

Integration of Logic and Behavior

This blending of logic and perceived value is called "praxeology" which was first discovered by the Greek philosophers. It is concerned with the conceptual analysis and logical implications of preference and choice. Over the years, praxeology was extended to form the basis of economics and social science. Therefore, a perceived value needs to be found at the intersection of the logic and behavioral influences.

Truly successful individuals and organizations use this approach when planning a major change. Feeling and emotion are equally important as the use of hard logic and reasoning. It is at the intersection of these perspectives where the best solution can be found.

During the planning and execution of the change initiative, the solution must be chunked into short duration milestones to maintain a sense of control over the changing circumstances. Change efforts fail, not because of the amount of change, but the fear of losing control. Individuals are constantly experiencing change and can quickly adapt. They feel threatened when they believe they no longer have a choice. Short term milestones help provide that sense of control.

I have found some great references that can provide in-depth information: Simon Sinek is the author of *Start with Why: How Great Leaders Inspire Everyone to Take Action.* Mr. Sinek can also be found on TED Talks. Roy Sutherland explains Praxeology in his TED Talk entitled Perspective *is everything.*

50

Process Improvement Using Trial and Error

*"Action and reaction, ebb and flow, trial and error, change -
this is the rhythm of living. Out of our over-confidence, fear;
out of our fear, clearer vision, fresh hope, and out of hope,
progress."*

— Bruce Barton

I N A RAPIDLY changing world, innovation is becoming a key differentiator. Process Innovation is about generating, evaluating, and implementing creative solutions that enable Process Excellence.

Below are seven heuristics that can be used to generate process innovation options. (A heuristic, according to Webster, is an aid to learning, discovery, or problem-solving by experimenting especially using trial-and-error methods)

These heuristics are also known as the Seven R's which represent seven dimensions or elements of a process that can be changed.

- **Rethink** (why) - the rationale and assumptions behind processes and their outcomes.
- **Reconfigure** (what) - the activities involved.
- **Reassign** (who) - the process performers.
- **Re-sequence** (when) - the timing and sequencing of work.
- **Relocate** (where) - the location and physical infrastructure.
- **Reduce** (how much) - the frequency of activities.
- **Retool** (how) - the technologies and competencies that enable work to be done.

By using these heuristics, process designers can discover new approaches and create new processes. In practice, a change made to one dimension of a process will typically affect several others. Example: if work is *reassigned* to a supplier, the work may also be *relocated* to the supplier's place of business. In addition, the process might be *retooled* with new technologies to link the organization and the supplier. For each heuristic, there are a number of questions designed to encourage fresh approaches and prompt perspectives.

The questions for each heuristic are not a comprehensive list or a "quality assurance" checklist. They are intended to demonstrate ways that a process designer might consider and examine a process in order to improve it. In practice, process professionals will undoubtedly find additional questions and perspectives that help identify improvement opportunities. When generating ideas, keep the following three points in mind:

1. Always consider three or more options---this raises the likelihood of developing a truly innovative solution. Do not jump too quickly to "the answer."

2. Think "and" rather than "or"---good ideas are seldom mutually exclusive.

3. Separate idea generation from idea evaluation. Sometimes the most outlandish idea turns out to be right. To avoid eliminating such ideas prematurely, ban any judging of ideas in the early stages of idea creation. Give people time to ponder, to imagine, to get used to an idea.

THE SEVEN HEURISTICS FOR PROCESS IMPROVEMENT

While there is no guaranteed formula for creativity, there are approaches and techniques that can be used to design and implement new and better processes. These approaches are embodied in the following seven heuristics and their associated questions.

1. **RETHINK (Why)**
   - What is the root cause of the problem?
   - What are the reasons for doing it this way?
   - What are the assumptions or rules underlying the current model? Are they true? Do they have to be true?
   - Is this process valuable enough to continue?

2. **RECONFIGURE (What)**
   - How can the entire activity be eliminated?
   - How can common activities be consolidated?
   - How can reconciliation be reduced by putting quality at the source?
   - How can information sharing with suppliers and customers improve the process?
   - How can intermediaries and non-value-adding work be eliminated?
   - How can best practices from other industries be borrowed and improved upon?

3. **REASSIGN (Who)**
   - How can existing activities and decisions be moved to a different organization?

- How can the activity be outsourced?
- How can the customer perform this activity?
- How can the organization perform an activity that the customer is currently performing?
- How can cross-training integrate and compress tasks?
- How can suppliers/partners perform this activity?

4. **RESEQUENCE (When)**
   - How can predicting increase efficiency?
   - How can postponement increase flexibility?
   - How can the number of interconnections and dependencies be minimized?
   - How can parallelism reduce time?

5. **RELOCATE (Where)**
   - How can the activity be moved closer to the customer or supplier to improve the effectiveness?
   - How can the activity be moved closer to related activities to improve communication?
   - How can we decrease the cycle time by reducing travel time and distance?
   - How can geographically virtual organizations be created?

6. **REDUCE (How Much)**
   - How can the frequency of the activity be reduced or increased?
   - How can critical resources be used more effectively?
   - How would less information or fewer controls simplify and improve efficiency?
   - How would more information enable greater effectiveness?

7. **RETOOL (How)**
   - How can technology transform the process?
   - How can the activity be automated?

- How can assets or competencies be leveraged to create competitive advantage?
- How can up-skilling, down-skilling, or multi-skilling improve the process?

Keep in mind that changes in a process may have an impact on technical capabilities. Technology may be able to enhance the process by providing greater efficiencies. Process changes also change the way the employees work and the number of people needed to support the process. The prevailing organizational culture can greatly influence the way in which processes and jobs are designed and how people interact with others to perform their work.

51

LESSONS LEARNED FROM MAJOR CHANGE INITIATIVES

*"I stopped thinking about it after trying to figure out what are
the lessons learned, and there are so many. After I had basically
sorted that out, I figured it's time to really look at the future
and not at the past."*

— KALPANA CHAWLA

A S AN EXPERIENCED consultant, I have studied what makes a large-scale change initiative successful. I would like to share a composite project to illustrate where things can go wrong.

Bob, the Chief Financial Officer and Sarah, the Director of I.T. led an effort to improve financial controls around business units and to consolidate reporting. After some investigation, it was determined that an upgrade to their existing enterprise systems would satisfy their needs. The business case was put forward to the Board resulting in an approved budget.

A tier 1 consulting company was contracted based on their ability to successfully implement the application. Selected subject matter experts from the business units along with other support personnel were chosen to form the project team. Although these employees were assigned to the project, they were still responsible for their assigned work.

Project plans and schedules were developed by the consulting group, and the planning phase was started. The team became familiar with the new features and functionalities and then set out to gather the business requirements needed to configure the application. The technical team worked on setting up the infrastructure to support the expanded capability of the application and planned interfaces to the legacy applications.

When the departmental managers became aware of the new features and functionality of the system, they raised some concerns. The managers were asked to validate and approve the requirements that defined the operation of the application. In order to control costs, the CFO and IT director agreed that custom coding would not be allowed. Since the application handled processes different from current practices, managers were reluctant to make decisions and grant approval to proceed with the configuration. This unwillingness to agree with the new functionality created delays in the schedule.

As efforts were made to resolve differences, more managers were discovering that business processes between departments and business units were inconsistent. Some departments provided well-documented policies, processes, and procedures while others offered little if any documentation. Since the application required a consistent standard, greater pushback was encountered by the managers. These managers were opposed to creating uniform standards, citing unique differences in their activities. Project tasks were focused on creating a standard to be used across the organization, but that became a lengthy ordeal that often dove into specific details which sidetracked the team.

The new automated features and workflow capabilities greatly impact specific job roles. Many of the tasks that employees performed on a routine basis were now being automated, no longer requiring to be completed manually. Business rules were also incorporated into the system eliminating the need for employees and managers to make certain decisions. This perceived loss of control created a great deal of stress.

Project costs were mounting with the unexpected delays. The project team did not anticipate or plan for delays of this magnitude. The project manager along with the CFO and I.T. director made the decision to bring on more staff and extend the timeframe.

When the consulting group started to develop end user training, they discovered that the employees did not have the same competency level for the same job role across the organization. In order to proceed, each person that performed a specific job needed to have a baseline skill and knowledge level before learning how to use the new application.

Faced with mounting changes in job roles, staffing levels, policy changes, and training, the decision was made to narrow the scope of the project until there was an agreement across the organization. When the initiative was completed, the budget exceeded the forecast by one-third, time frames also exceeded the projected forecast by twenty-five percent, and the scope was drastically reduced.

What lessons can we learn from this experience?

1. We know that technology is rapidly advancing and can be a very effective tool that can improve operational performance, but it is still a tool and part of a larger, integrated solution.
2. The People and organizational systems, business processes, and knowledge Management are also drivers of performance and need to be integrated and aligned to achieve the desired results.
3. The business capabilities must be aligned and support the proposed solution.
4. Forecasting project budgets and timeframes are almost always underestimated by at least twenty-five percent.

52

COMMUNICATING CHANGE EFFECTIVELY

"When you really listen to another person from their point of view and reflect back to them that understanding, it's like giving them emotional oxygen."

— STEPHEN COVEY

EVERYONE KNOWS THAT communicating change is critical for buy-in and support. But the approach that is often used gets the message lost in translation. Change management turns into a set of tasks with defined deliverables. This may be needed for project plans, but it fails to achieve the desired results.

The bottom-up approach to organizational change management is a common technique used by change management practitioners to ensure each stakeholder understands and is prepared for change. The activities in the bottom-up approach generally start by conducting a stakeholder assessment to determine the type and degree of change that impacts that individual. Then, a communication plan is developed outlining a specific set of key messages delivered at specified times throughout the project. To coincide with the communication is a training plan to learn new skills so the employee can perform their job. This type of change management is good for small, targeted change such as preparing for an upgrade to Microsoft Office, but fails as an effective solution to manage a large-scale transformational change because it attempts to force a change of an individual into an environment that has already changed.

Here is an analogy to illustrate my point: Jim and Sue had purchased their home eight years ago in a community they knew well. The couple had fallen into a routine, getting up at 6:00 AM, commuting 30 minutes to work Monday through Friday, returning home at 5:00 PM, eating dinner an hour later, then settle in for the evening watching their favorite TV shows or reading a book. Many of their neighbors were close friends and enjoyed weekend barbecues and holiday parties. The shopping area was close by as well as the parks and libraries. The couple had planned to remain in the area for a long time.

One day, the reports on the radio called for severe storms. As the day went on the storms drew closer and with frequent warnings on the TV and radio. The storm intensified that evening with high winds and hail. When the Tornado siren sounded, Jim took Sue into their basement. They were frightened as the winds tore through their community. When they emerged several hours later, their home was severely damaged; their neighbors home along with others were completely destroyed. With no lights or distinguishing landmarks, they felt lost in their front yard. A police officer came by and directed the couple to walk to the corner where a bus would pick them up. Jim asked where it would take them, but the officer said he didn't know and left to continue his investigation. Everything in the neighborhood was destroyed. In the days and weeks that followed, city officials would provide direction but could not provide a long-term plan. Everything had changed: many of their friends were not seen again; their home unlivable, and the stores gone. Information was provided to them only after plans were in place. Jim and Sue were forced to change to fit into a new living environment. They were given specific communication about key events. Throughout their ordeal, there was no clearly articulated vision or where they allowed participate in the decisions that were being made in their lives. Jim and Sue were frustrated and confused.

This is how bottom-up change management is managed in many organizations. The employees are managed through a process without a clear vision of why, how, and what will change. Then, the employees are fit in after the change has occurred and expected to perform as usual. The employees are not considered part of the change initiative, but rather expected to listen to the key messages, comprehend what is being said, and then conform to the change that has taken place. Change management is not just communication and skills training. Communication, by definition, is the act or process of using words, sounds, signs, and behaviors to express or exchange information, thoughts, and feelings to some else. However, it has turned into a very structured and methodical way of telling a select group of people a specific limited message at a specific time.

A top-down change management approach like Dr. John Kotter's Eight Steps starts with describing what the senior leadership believes to be true and continues to articulate a clear vision for the future. As the change vision is driven down from the strategic level to the tactical, operational, and functional levels within the organization, it transforms into actionable events. The change vision should describe the goals in measurable and actionable terms. A common mistake is made when the vision is described as implementing a new enterprise software solution. This does not describe the business problem or define how the business will operate in the future. If the change vision is to become more responsive to customers, then the vision should describe how the business processes will change, how the technologies, will enhance the processes and reduce manual administrative tasks, determine what information is needed, and describe how employee behaviors need to change to create a better customer experience.

The change communication from a top-down approach is incorporated into every activity from understanding the business problem, to aligning the people, process, technology and information to realize the change vision.

53

BEING SECURE AND SAFE

"Let not him who is houseless pull down the house of another, but let him work diligently and build one for himself, thus by example assuring that his own shall be safe from violence when built."

— ABRAHAM LINCOLN

DESPITE ALL OF the safety and security policies that are enforced within the workplace, security breaches, accidents and injuries still continue to be a major concern for management. End users are said to be the weakest link in security systems in the workplace. They often knowingly engage in certain activities that violate security policies without malicious intentions. Unsafe behaviors, not conditions, account for more than 90 percent of injuries in the United States. Traditional safety programs, however, often focus on conditions and ignore behaviors. I will describe a few situations that led to a breach of security and safety policies that created issues and then I will identify some of the key causes that led to these incidents.

Lost Security

An internet marketing company located in the heart of a busy city needed to implement new security controls to comply with heightened financial regulatory requirements. Security cameras were installed throughout the complex including the lobby. Employees were issued electronic security cards with card readers in the lobby and other key access points. The building was secure from any unauthorized person from entering the building. There was a door in the rear of the office that led to an alley. The employees would leave the door open to get fresh air and to get to the fast food restaurant down the street, or to take a cigarette break. Nothing was ever said by the managers since this open door was convenient to so many people, and it saved time from going all the way to the front entrance. One day, an employee reported a laptop was missing from the manager's office. A thorough investigation was conducted, and it was determined that a well-dressed man claiming to be a consultant walked right into the office in front of many employees and took the computer. Everyone assumed that the person was just doing their job since he did not look like a thief. Employees did not question the stranger since he appeared to be confident and was dress appropriately. Everyone made the assumption that robberies took place at night.

A Killer Decision

An aircraft maintenance facility had fallen behind in their scheduled prevention and repairs on the aircraft. This had become a big issue that needed to be resolved quickly. Management devised a plan that would incentivize employees. Individuals were formed into small teams and provided a work schedule. Each team negotiated the amount of time it would take to complete the assigned task. The plan would reward employees if they completed tasks ahead of schedule with a large cash incentive. One day a plane came in with unscheduled maintenance to replace a fuel pump in the wing. A team was assigned the task but were upset because they knew they might not receive the incentive bonus. Since the aircraft arrived toward the end of their work shift, they decided to tackle the project the following day. Determined, one team member decided to start the task in hopes to get the incentive pay. Working without a supervisor for his safety, he picked up the specialized tools and entered the fuel tank where the pump was located. His teammate who was in the hanger realized something was wrong and went to help his partner who was unconscious. Once removed from the compartment resuscitation efforts were attempted but failed. An initial investigation of the company determined that the employee failed to follow documented safety procedures which led to his death. An independent investigation found that the reward was a greater incentive than the safety risk. The employees did not work as a unified team which allowed one employee to work on their own. There was no policy that made accommodation for non-scheduled work. It was the large cash reward and the lack of defined policies that drove a dangerous change in behavior.

In each of these cases, the behaviors of employees led to a loss of property and a loss of life. What would be so influencing that would change behaviors especially when measures are taken to prevent negative consequences? Behaviors are influenced by the environment, in which the employees work such as leadership and managerial styles, policies, and rewards. Leaders need to convey the vision and need for employees, so they understand the reason for the directive. Policies need to be written to set specific rules to guide employees in the way they perform their tasks. Rewards should be used along with punishments. A reward such as cash has a powerful influence on altering behavior, but when the reward becomes excessive, it will cause employees to take risks. If there is no punishment, then the reward becomes an entitlement and will no longer be an incentive to change.

54

THE RULES THAT KILLED A BUSINESS

"Complaining is dangerous business. It can damage or even destroy your relationship with God, your relationships with other people, and even with your relationship with yourself."

— JOYCE MEYER

THE HUDSON ELECTRIC Service Company opened its doors in a small garage on the Southwest side of Chicago in 1927. The company built and repaired electric motors for commercial and industrial use. The business was steady as local companies began to prosper after the world war. The president and founder of the company believed in hard work and attention to detail. The president could be found on the shop floor more often than in his office. His work values and participative involvement in shop floor activities flourished among the other employees. Hudson's reputation for quality and service became a benchmark as the company grew.

The employees at the young company adopted the same work ethic as the management team. The employees knew that with the hard work, they would get recognized and rewarded for their effort. If a customer had an urgent request to repair a motor, the workers would work well beyond their normal shift to complete the job. Although this did not often occur, it was however expected. Employees did not expect to be paid overtime because they knew that there were times when there was little to do, and the shop supervisor allowed them to go home early. This situation made the employees satisfied with their pay and working conditions.

Throughout the 1930's the federal government was focused on labor relations and fair employment standards. These new regulations established the new 40-hour workweek and defined the minimum wage. Although the employees were well paid, the federal standard for hours worked within a week changed the way employees approached their job. With the new regulation, the focus shifted from doing what it took to get the job done, to what they could do within an 8-hour day.

Now, any work that exceeded a forty-hour work week required the company to pay overtime wages. It became difficult to manage the employee's time when they were allowed to leave work early when there was little work. As a result, the company established more formal working hours, defining when employees had to start and stop work. A time-clock was added to allow employees to punch in and out to comply with the new federal regulation.

Some employees started to feel that management no longer trusted them which at times created frustration and tension. At that time, employees were paid what the job was worth, and other outside standards did not determine it. The candidate and Hudson's management would come to an agreement as to the type of work, the wage, and the duration. This worked well for many prospective employees who just wanted a chance to prove their worth, or to earn some quick money. Once the terms were agreed to, there were no other expectations or entitlements. The job may have been the completion of a one-time task, such as cleaning out a storage room, or it may have been a task which may only require a few hours per week. When the minimum wage regulation commenced, the focus changed from job worth to employee entitlement. As a result, the management at Hudson could not hire new employees until such time there was enough work to justify paying the increased wage.

However, with the state and federal regulations, it became cost prohibitive for the company, and these candidates expected a steady, full-time income. As a result, those extra tasks were delegated to other employees.

The minimum wage increased nearly each year, starting at 25 cents per hour to 40 cents per hour in 1940. In 1949, the minimum wage took a drastic jump, increasing to 75 cents per hour, and by 1955 the rate was one dollar per hour. The behaviors of employees changed from getting paid for comparable work, to an entitlement to getting paid to support their lifestyle.

In addition to the federal employment standards, the new Social Security Act required employers to participate in an excise tax per employee based on a percentage of their wages. It was now becoming even more costly for the company to hire and maintain employees.

By 1947, the company had expanded from the small garage to an entire city block and operated a fleet of delivery trucks. However, the mandated regulations were just not confined to employers and employees. Local, state and federal regulations mandated changes in workplace conditions in the name of fairness, safety, and health. Hudson was more than just a place to work; it was a lifestyle. Employees were considered friends, with their motto, "work hard and play hard". The president would host picnics at his house for the friends of the company. There would be holiday parties as well as after work social events such as bowling or baseball. Employees were happy, safe, and loyal.

With each passing year, the cost of complying with the new requirements steadily increased. The tipping point came in 1970 when the city of Chicago declared that the old unused water tank on the roof of the building along with a tall chimney that was also no longer used appeared to be a safety hazard and needed to be removed. The cost of removing these structures was extreme and could not be sustained by Hudson. The company was forced into bankruptcy and closed their doors for good in 1972. For many of the 278 employees, Hudson was their only job.

Regulations for business are needed to ensure the health and safety of employees and their customers. However, these regulations should be used as a guideline and not to take the control away from the business leaders if they are achieving the same results in another way. Regulations have negative consequences as described in the story above. Therefore, the lesson learned is that a regulation, policy, or rule should not be enforced across the entire organization but rather be used as a guideline, allowing individual groups to establish their own standards of performance.

55

THE RIGHT PERSONALITY FOR THE JOB

"Always be yourself, express yourself, have faith in yourself, do not go out and look for a successful personality and duplicate it."

— BRUCE LEE

BUSINESS LEADERS MAKE an assumption that employees just need to be trained to perform new tasks after a large-scale change has taken place. This is a risky assumption, in that the changes that have occurred are not all based on learning a new skill. The generic vision of many large-scale change initiatives centers on increasing operational performance through automation, integration of systems, and efficient processes. Although new competencies are often associated with technical and process changes, the change required for specific roles may be more about a shift in behaviors rather than a specific skill. When there is a shift away from administrative tasks, to a more decision-making role, it requires a new set of behaviors. Employees that were assigned a specific role may not have the personality style needed to make tough decisions even though they have all of the required skills.

Lisa Smith is a department manager within accounts payable. She has worked for the company for six years and has been a very good employee. Lisa is very knowledgeable about the accounts payable process and took pride in the accuracy and timeliness of her work. It was this level of quality and devotion that got her promoted to department manager. Lisa has been a manager for the past year and supervises six accounts payable clerks.

The company was facing some tough economic conditions and has planned for a large-scale change initiative to reduce operational costs while improving customer service. At the center of this initiative was the installation of an enterprise software application which would integrate with other systems, automate tasks, provide workflow triggers, and provide accessibility to the customers through the internet.

Many of the accounts payable processes were impacted by the new software addition. Since the software was able to capture paper and electronic invoices automatically and triggered electronic invoice approval workflow for appropriate approvals, it eliminated many of the manual tasks performed by the payroll clerks. In addition, the enterprise software allowed department managers to have more control over their employees by providing many of the tasks that once were the responsibility of human resources, such as providing merit raises, authorizing transfers, and even termination requests.

Lisa's role was changing significantly with the increase in responsibility and authority of specifying payment parameters and approving invoices for payments. In the past, Lisa ensured that all of the accounts payable tasks were performed on time. Establishing payment terms, approving invoices were the responsibility of the Comptroller. Hiring and terminating employees was the job of the human resources manager. Now, Lisa was tasked to become a decision-maker, moving away from performing the administrative tasks that she was accustomed to doing.

The department was actively involved in configuring and testing the new software and redesigning accounts payable processes. It became clear to Lisa that the new functionality may not require as many people to perform the tasks. She assumed that if, in fact, there was a staffing change that the senior leaders would take care of them. Lisa's first assignment after the system went live was to reduce her staff by fifty percent. It was up to Lisa to identify and terminate those employees. This was an agonizing proposition since Lisa had worked alongside these people since she started six years earlier and considered them close friends. The process of selecting three staff members weighed heavy on her mind. She had sought support from senior leaders in finance and human resources, but they empathized with her and gave her moral encouragement. Weeks had passed without making a decision on who would go and who would stay. Finally, the Comptroller took charge and together with Lisa, dismissed the three employees.

Negotiating payment terms also became a challenge for Lisa as she worked with suppliers who resisted change. Very little was done to change the terms for long standing suppliers that the company had done business with over the years. Lisa did not want for them to threaten the delivery of supplies to the company due to payment disputes and jeopardize the company's operation. The comptroller had to step into meetings with Lisa to assist in resolving a heated exchange.

The same issue occurred over approving invoices for various departments. Lisa did not want a confrontation with department managers who were senior with to her and yielded more clout with the executives. Each time she tried to challenge a questionable invoice she was met with resistance. They would tell Lisa that she did not know how operations worked and then she would doubt herself.

After six months after the new initiative went live, Lisa found herself struggling to maintain her position. She was stressed, and it was apparent in the quality of her work. Out of the three remaining AP clerks, one had resigned, and the other was visibly upset and was seeking a transfer. The senior management realized that Lisa could not perform the new tasks and was demoted to the AP clerk position after her replacement was found.

In reflection of this situation, employees who are exceptional at performing their job tasks often get promoted to a position that requires a new set of competencies and behaviors. Lisa was well qualified as an AP clerk, with the years of experience and knowledge she was "technically" qualified to perform the job of a manager. Her old position did not require her to make tough decisions or have negotiation skills needed for her new role. The redesigned manager role required new behaviors that can't be taught. As a result, the requirements of the new role were no longer a match to Lisa's qualifications.

56

THE KNOWLEDGE OF
KNOWLEDGE MANAGEMENT

*"Knowledge has to be improved, challenged, and increased
constantly, or it vanishes."*

— PETER DRUCKER

WE OFTEN TALK about knowledge management in terms of reports and business intelligence tools to promote analysis of information. However, knowledge management is much more than reporting and analysis software applications. Knowledge management is not another word for business intelligence. There are defined methodologies and proven approaches that are adopted by organizations that aid in fostering knowledge. The purpose of this article is to simplify the concept of knowledge management in order to incorporate this information into transformation initiatives. There are five Knowledge management levels: data, information, understanding, knowledge, and wisdom.

Data: Data is a single piece of information, by itself is meaningless. Data could be a name, a number, a date, or any figure that is collected. Bill Jones, $120.00, and Milwaukee are examples of data and does not have a meaning to the user until it is placed into context. The source of the data can be critical to the accuracy of the data. In many cases there may be several sources to draw the data; the actual data itself may not be exact. The sources of the data may not have malicious intent, but rather not be timely; they may have obtained information from another source. Therefore, everyone must agree on the source of the information.

Information: Information is a sequence of related data that is placed into context. The names, titles, phone numbers and email addresses of corporate officers are an example of information. Data on yearly sales revenue, number of employees, stock prices, plant locations, and product descriptions are combined to create a profile of the business which can be used for targeting marketing campaigns, granting credit, and many other purposes. When the data used to create this profile is inaccurate, it could cause people to make wrong decisions.

Understanding: Understanding is having the mental grasp and the capability to comprehend the general relations of the particulars. In other words, based upon a person's comprehension of the information that is matched to similar experiences from their past that they believe are true, that person therefore may be able to make sense of the information presented to them within their specific context. Jane understands for example that she has to complete a sequence of tasks, correctly, and in a specific order to complete the sales transaction for the customer. The price data on the item must match that data entered into the cash register. Jane compares the information on the customer's driver's license to that on the check. She understands that if the information on the check does not match the driver's license, then there could be a possibility of fraud.

Knowledge: Knowledge is taking the understanding of information and using it for a specific purpose. As new Knowledge is acquired through education, learning, and experiencing, it can evolve and change over time. So therefore knowledge is subject to revision based upon current theory and practice.

Business leaders often rely on a mastery of knowledge through certifications or formal academic degrees. They use this as a baseline that qualifies a person to fulfill job role requirements. Based upon the understanding of the customer requirements, and the employees professional certification in the field, the proposed solution that was offered my not work in this particular situation because the manufacturer changed the formula.

Wisdom: Wisdom is the ability to make correct judgments and decisions. It is an intangible quality gained presumably through experience. Knowledge is what you know; wisdom is the capacity to judge. Wisdom is knowing what to know, how much and what to do with it. Knowledge is obtained; wisdom is developed. However, it appears that many business leaders do not place a great deal of value in wisdom, and primarily look for the person who can perform the assigned tasks without questioning or altering the process. But yet, that is exactly what organizations strive to do, that is, to improve performance and quality. Based on the employee's education and experience working with similar businesses, time and cost savings could be realized if the process was changed by reassigning these tasks and using mobile devices to record the transactions.

Here is another way to think of these levels of knowledge management, by answering three questions: "What" needs to be done, "How" do we perform the job better, and" Why" do we perform the job that way. It is easy to tell people what we do, such as, we sell tools to the retail market, or we provide accounting services to individuals and small businesses. I am a cashier, or I am an accountant is a common way we use to describe our job because other people generally have an "understanding" of those job roles. It becomes a bit more difficult to describe "how" we perform those jobs. Individuals who may not have experience or knowledge of the job activities may not comprehend how the work activities are different. The "why" question is the most difficult to answer but yet the most important question for people to understand. The "why" question describes what individuals believe to be true. This question is the sole reason for an organization's existence. This is what differentiates the organization or the individual from all the rest.

When an organization is able to capture the wisdom, they are able to have a synergistic belief in knowing that they are doing something that has a meaningful purpose that will add value to their customers, employees, and the community at large. The customers will also be able to connect to the organization's vision and beliefs.

57

Effective Collaboration for Change

*"Teamwork is the ability to work together toward a common
vision. The ability to direct individual accomplishments toward
organizational objectives. It is the fuel that allows common
people to attain uncommon results."*

— Andrew Carnegie

O N MANY WEBSITES where a request for information is required, the user
is often asked to enter a system generated word that is often written
in a way that is artistic with distorted wavy letters. That program is called
CAPTCHA, which is an acronym meaning Completely Automated Public
Turing test to tell Computers and Humans Apart. CAPTCHA is used to differentiate a human from a computer, that the user is actually a person that is
accessing information. This program prevents computer programs from automatically purchasing tickets, accessing personal information, taking a survey
or a host of other information. Technology has not currently advanced to the
point where a computer can identify and translate a cryptic graphic of letters

and place them in the correct place in the right order to unlock the security to gain access to the application.

We as humans go through a similar process when we validate that other individuals meet our qualifications to collaborate. Collaboration is the ability to work together to do a task to achieve a common goal. Therefore, in order for us to effectively collaborate we instinctively go through a validation process. Unlike the CAPTCHA program where it validates the task of a human correctly typing the cryptic letters into a field, individuals use a series of validations that determines their level of comfort and trust to share information, work together, and have a similar understanding of the goal.

The first validation occurs within the first 3 minutes of meeting an individual for the first time. The first validation point is the ability to interact effectively. Physical appearance, stance, and demeanor are the first acceptance gates. To illustrate this point, Doctor Gottman, a researcher conducted several studies where an audience had 3 minutes to observe the interaction of several newly married couples to predict if they would end up divorced. The audience observed their behaviors and listened how they communicated with each other. The study revealed an accuracy rate of 94%. Therefore, when individuals first meet, each person is assessing the way they communicate - the words they use, the tone, volume, and inflection. Body language is also a clear indicator - their posture, the distance between the two people, eye contact, and the use of their hands. In Dr. Gottman's study, the participants could instinctively tell the commitment and compatibility of the couples within a very short period of time.

The second validation stage is the assessment of common knowledge and experiences. This starts when individuals engage in conversation to assess their understanding of common goals and objectives. Their understanding is having the mental grasp and the capability to comprehend the general relations of the particulars. In other words, based upon a person's comprehension of the information that is matched to similar experiences from their past that they believe are true, that person therefore may be able to make sense of the information presented to them within their specific context. If the individuals do not have an understanding of the terminology, methods, models, and approaches, then it would be difficult to achieve true collaboration.

To achieve true collaboration, it requires more than just sharing common experiences, but rather collectively developing core knowledge of the situation, goals, and objectives. Since knowledge is viewed as understanding how information is used for a specific purpose, new knowledge is acquired through situational awareness and learning and experiencing how the concepts can effectively be applied to the new situation to accomplish the stated goal. Collaboration does not mean that the participants must agree on every aspect. Differences of opinion often provoke thought and different perspectives. Leadership is used to build consensus around a clearly defined vision to reach the goal.

Collaboration must overcome political or philosophical differences to achieve the desired results. This is easier said than done. However, this is where strong leadership is required. The goals can be achieved when the vision describes the desired outcomes of the collaboration effort. Team members can actually approach the problem from opposite perspectives and still reach a common goal when the desired outcomes are defined.

During a large-scale change initiative, it is common to have differing points of view. Project team members will often have experiences and competencies even when they are working in similar roles. Individuals develop expectations based on their past experiences. These expectations can be dissimilar which will create outcomes that may not align with the transformational goals expected by senior leadership. When change leaders create a clearly defined change vision, it paints a picture of what the future looks like. The vision can define the expectations for team members to establish a starting point for collaboration.

58

BUSINESS CONTINUITY AND
LARGE SCALE CHANGE

"Just because the river is quiet does not mean the crocodiles have left."

— MALAY PROVERB

BUSINESS CONTINUITY AND disaster recovery are often far from the minds of senior leaders as they plan for a major change initiative. However, the business continuity and disaster recovery plan should be part of the overall strategic plan for business transformation. The focus should be more than just the organization's ability to recover data and restore systems. Changes in the technical capabilities, information sharing and knowledge management, business processes, organization and people all have a major impact on how the continuity of business and the immediate recovery is managed.

Litton Pharmaceuticals is a 32-year-old generic marketer of generic branded and Over-the-Counter products in more than 30 countries. In an effort to increase market penetration, the senior leadership decided to undertake a large-scale transformation initiative that would create virtual offices, allowing representatives to conduct business via the cloud using tablets. In addition, suppliers and medical facilities would have access to the site allowing them greater accessibility anytime of the day.

The project had taken nearly a year and a half with the guidance of a consulting company. The focus of the project was setting up service-oriented architecture to provide a web-based solution. Many of their essential business applications had to be replaced or extensively changed to meet the new mobile requirements while ensuring data security. Business processes were adjusted to accommodate the new technology, and the employees were trained to navigate the applications on their new tablets.

The transition to the new web-based application went relatively smooth considering the scope of the project. There were some glitches in the workflow as they transitioned from paper to electronic forms. Many of the work triggers and approvals were set up through email while other tasks that were out of scope were still handled manually. Although some activities were not identified during the project, the business leaders worked out the known issues.

Seven months after the system go-live, the small community where the company was located was severely damaged by a 6.2 magnitude earthquake. The office building was damaged along with the homes of many of the managers that lived in the nearby community. Although there was no life loss, many residents had sustained injuries. Power lines and other structures were knocked down blocking the roadways. In the days that followed, the recovery process continued on the path to regain normalcy.

Litton's failover systems had worked well and only one day of data was actually lost. The backup servers located in a different state continued to operate. The physical building was damaged and needed to be inspected for safety before employees could return. Since many of the manager's homes were also damaged, they were not able or willing to return to work until their safety and security were restored. As a result, they were not able to approve requests, or make decisions that were needed to operate the day-to-day business. The business continuity plan that was developed years ago was filed in the Chief Operating Officers desk which now was under a pile of rubble. Since key decision-makers were not available, the business came to a halt. In an attempt to restore the business over the following weeks, the outdated business continuity plan was no longer workable since the business processes were changed along with the reporting relationships and roles. Although the customers could place orders and request information through the website, and the account representatives could take orders, the back office operations failed to function. The business processes that were changed to meet the transformation vision were not tested and validated under the business continuity plan. The business faced a significant financial loss because of their inability to operate.

At the strategic level of a business transformation initiative, the change vision is the driving factor. But, does the proposed change align with the business continuity and disaster recovery plan? The ability to recover critical business data is important to the survival of the business. However, when Litton moved to conduct business in the cloud through tablets that changed the way the data would be accessed. Business continuity and disaster recovery planning must be strategic tasks as part of any business transformation effort. Any time that technical systems, business processes, organizational structures, reporting relationships, job roles, and policies are changed, as part of a large-scale change initiative, then the business continuity and disaster recovery plan must be reviewed to determine any potential impact.

59

LOST IN TRANSLATION

"You don't die if you fall into the water; you only die if you don't swim."

— UNKNOWN AUTHOR

THERE ARE TIMES in conversation with friends and family when we talk about one thing, and the other person misinterprets what we are discussing. When it is realized, we laugh and continue talking. Issues arise when we are giving important directions to a person, and they misinterpret the meaning. I have found that to be the case in large-scale projects I have worked. People from many disciplines come together to achieve a single goal, on-time, and within budget. However, what we say can be misconstrued resulting in work being performed that is undesired and resulting in damaging consequences.

Here is a fun example of the use of slang used on a project: The consultants on an engagement used a SME to create a straw man where we could leverage the data for the chargeable deck. We had an hour before our hard stop at the EOD. The side conversations were taken offline. We did not want to boil the ocean with the 20,000-foot view, so we put the information into logical buckets without doing any deep dives. We just had to wordsmith and tighten up a few things before the deliverable was due; it was a good takeaway. The SME was a rock star and totally bought into the MECE approach. We rolled off the project and now we are on the beach.

Someone not familiar with consultant ease may not understand what was just said. I will translate what the consultants were discussing. The consultants on a contract assignment used an employee that is experienced in a specific area of business, or subject matter expert to create a conceptual model that can be easily rebutted by others, where we could use the appropriate information for the PowerPoint presentation that is a billable deliverable. We had an hour before our required completion time at the end of the day. The side conversations were curtailed until after the meeting. We did not want to address all of the related topics with the high-level view, so we grouped the information without providing details. We just had to make spelling corrections and rewrite some sentences before the deliverable was due; the facts we provided were very informative. The subject matter expert was very good and totally accepted the choice of topic groups that were mutually exclusive and collectively exhaustive. We rolled off the project and now we are awaiting our next assignment.

This type of talk may sound slick and can be confusing to others, but this slang and shorthand conversation are not limited to consultants, in fact almost every group has their own terminology. The finance department uses terms like book value, EBIT, KPI's, and P-cards while the I.T. department uses other terms like bridge, cookies, domains, FTP and GUI. However, the unique terminology that is shared among functional areas within the project will be identified and learned. The learning process generally does not take that long since everyone that is involved in the project is aware of the differences and works hard to understand. The problem occurs when words that seem to be common between functional areas are used but have a different meaning.

A more serious example that creates confusion and frustration is the terminology around the word, "Process". This is a word that is used in different functional areas and has a slightly different meaning that could have negative consequences for the project.

A staff employee may define a process as a series of work steps to bring about a result. This describes the details needed to perform a task.

An I.T. employee may think data flow from one system to another as a process.

An executive may think of the process as the value chain that describes the end-to-end functionality of the business operation.

A program manager may think of business process reengineering, where a radical change in the business provides value to the customer.

A project manager may think of business process redesign needed to change work activities that are generally changed from new technology capabilities.

A quality manager may think of business process improvement is needed to make incremental changes to work activities.

An applications specialist may think business process alignment is needed to adjust the process to meet the new technical features and functionality.

When a process change is required within a project, the leadership should not take for granted that project team members all have the same understanding and perspective. These individuals have a comfort level with their interpretation and approach to a process which may not address the requirements of the project.

To ensure that everyone that works on the project or who is directly impacted by the outcome of the project should have a clear understanding of what is being conveyed, it should not be taken for granted. One solution is to create a glossary of terms that is accessible to all of the stakeholders. Project team members should also refrain from using slang or words that are unique to that group or functional area.

60

RESISTING CHANGE

*"People often resist change for reasons that make good sense
to them, even if those reasons don't correspond to organizational goals. So it is crucial to recognize, reward and celebrate
accomplishments."*

— ROSABETH MOSS KANTER

THERE WAS A great deal of resistance to change among the mailroom staff
at a state government agency where a large-scale change initiative was
taking place. The organization was implementing a new financial system
including a new document scanner located in the mailroom that would make
it easy to search and verify the contents of the mail that was received by a
certain date.

Opening, sorting, and scanning mail was part of the mailroom staff responsibility. The new scanners added one more step in the process. During
time trials, this additional task added between 20 - 30 seconds to the overall
process and 5 minutes for the entire day. The business leaders were pleased

that the change would not have a noticeable change. The mailroom staff picked up this new task right away and performed it nearly perfectly the first time they attempted the new task.

The current layout had work tables arranged like desks where each mailroom employee personalized their own space with pictures of their family and friends. To accommodate the new scanners and to streamline the process, the desks and tables had to be rearranged. What came next was unexpected to the management team. The mailroom staff became very resistant to change. Their attitude became angry and tempers flared over little things. What was surprising to the managers was that that there was so much hostility over such a minor change.

Why would such a seemingly small change create such a negative reaction? When I explored the larger situation, it became evident why the mailroom employees resisted the change. The additional task was not the problem, neither was the rearrangement of their desks, these actions were just triggering events. The problem was much deeper and can be traced to the organizational culture. The state organization was very hierarchically controlled by the management. Lower level employees were not allowed to participate in a decision-making process which resulted in doing what they are told. It was common not to reward successes but to punish mistakes. The employees accepted that they had to be willing to obey orders, and work please their superiors to make the workplace tolerable. As a result, they did not want to get involved with special projects and waited for others to act first. Employees took very few chances and tried hard not to stand out or draw undue attention to themselves.

What were the signs? There were many subtle signs that were present when diagnosing the problem. First, it was quite clear to identify the management from the staff employees, as they had offices that were in another part of the building, far away from their staff. The supervisor was located in the corner, with a nice desk, surrounded by tall partitions while the staff members sat on wooden stools situated by long tables. Other than a few photographs taped to the wall, they did not have any drawers to store their personal items. Their tasks were quite clear with no opportunity to make recommendations for change. These staff employees were viewed as insignificant in the eyes of management, there to do a very specific task: open, sort, and scan incoming mail and nothing more. In conversations that were out of hearing range of the staff, managers would refer to these mail room clerks as "weeds" since they would pop up at unwanted times and would be annoying.

What created this culture? An organizational culture that promotes, trust, respect, and team participation starts with aligning the behaviors to those core values. It is incumbent upon the senior leadership team to reward those desired behaviors while punishing those who do not promote those same values. However, the focus on core values can become lost as the organization becomes more complex, and the demands of the business take priority. Responding to a crisis and shifting priorities, ensuring quality remains high despite using equipment that frequently breaks down and adapting to shrinking budgets are some reasons cited for the shift in behaviors. These leaders can shift from trust to mistrust, from respect to criticism, and from teams to individual control.

The mail room employees had very little control over their work and were told what to do and how to do it. The only thing they had control over was their space. When the project required moving tables around, their pictures and personal items were taken for granted and got lost in the shuffle. Their only thing they could call their own was now taken away. With nothing to lose, they revolted. The managers had no idea what created such turmoil and why they were acting this way. These employees were not treated as part of the team. It was their ability to open, sort and scan the mail that started the process, and it was up to the leadership team to recognize their contribution.

61

How Long Will It Really Take?

"Life does not obey our expectations. Life obeys our intentions, in ways we may not expect."

— Lloyd Strom

P ROJECTS RARELY SEEM to go as planned. Timeframes quickly change when a task doesn't get completed on time. Many of the large-scale projects that I have worked on have extended beyond the time by a factor of forty percent.

The plans have been formulated, and the stake was put in the ground for the completion date for the project. Based on expert opinion and major business events, with some room for slippage, the project team makes an agreement to the expected implementation of the new system on a date that is set in stone. Now, the project managers and leads put together their detailed task plan and work toward the defined milestones. Within a few short months, the project timeline is already being compromised with unanticipated issues: software licensing issues, staffing delays, and accessibility problems creep into the schedule. Although frustrating, the plan had some flexibility and hopes are high that the time will be saved in some other areas.

Now a few more months have passed, and the project plan is adjusted to meet the new timeline. As the problems were resolved, others popped up. One solution was to add more team members to the project to divide and conquer, but as yet no increase in efficiency had been made. The contingency time was used up and now the push to stay on target. There was not more room in the plan for setbacks to meet the target date.

Where does the time go? We often fall into a trap when planning our tasks. Within our project plan, we designate the elapsed time for a particular task, then link it to the next task, and so on. We feel that it will take five days to perform the work. But we know that we will not be working on that task without interruption. So many times, meetings are scheduled, other urgent tasks arise, and soon the elapsed working time is closer to ten days. Then the next task often does not start immediately following the previous task. There is a preparation that generally needs to take place. We finish the task at 4:30 PM and our workday ends at 5:00 PM. So, our tendency is to take a social break and prepare to start fresh the following morning.

There is a self-fulfilling prophesy regarding the performance of tasks within planned durations. A task is hardly ever completed ahead of schedule. There are several reasons for this. We can demonstrate these using a task that has a 50-50 chance of being completed in five days, but has been scheduled for ten days to allow for uncertainty, risk, emergency diversions, etc.

First, Parkinson's Law states that work expands so as to fill the time available for its completion". Work on the task has commenced on schedule and is essentially completed within the first five days. But, because ten days have been allocated for the task, the performer spends the next five days "fine tuning" the deliverable. This is a natural work ethic of most people. We reach 98% completion on our task and, if additional time is available, we attempt to refine it until a delivery deadline is reached.

Second, is the procrastination. We are able to start the task as scheduled. But, because there are ten days allocated, and we know that we only need five days, we wait a week to start the task. Now, of course, the contingency has been exhausted before the task has been started, and the potential for a schedule overrun has been increased. But, even if there are no problems, the five-day task has taken ten days.

Less obvious are the subtle motivators to avoid "early" completion of tasks. If we estimated ten days and completed the task in five days, we might be criticized for "padding" the estimate, even though the extra five days was a legitimate allowance for uncertainty. Or, we might be under increased pressure to shorten duration estimates in the future. There rarely is a reward for finishing tasks early– only demerits for running over. So where is the motivation to do the task in five days?

How can we adequately plan the completion time of a given task? The answer lies within the organization's culture. We can group behavioral styles together into four different cultures: constructive; bureaucratic; avoidant; and autocratic. An organization with a constructive style supports a balance between task and people. This type of culture usually is a team focused on encouraging and supporting each other to complete their assigned tasks. In a bureaucratic culture, employees conform to defined rules within a formal structure. These work silos create barriers from working together to achieve a common goal. Avoidant cultures support employees working independently to achieve their own goal, rarely relying on others to provide support. The autocratic culture places a focus on power and control. A competition is created between individuals and groups where there are winners and losers. Each one of these cultural differences has a big influence on completing tasks and achieving the goals of the project.

62

DOES YOUR JOB FIT YOU?

*"Choose a job you love, and you will never have to work a day
in your life."*

— CONFUCIUS

MANY LARGE-SCALE CHANGE projects will assign an Organizational Change Management specialist to address the communication and training needs of the stakeholders impacted by the initiative. The assumption is that these employees need to be informed of the changes, then trained to function in the transformed environment. However, situational awareness and skills training may not meet the competencies needed to support the newly transformed organization. As part of the transformation, there is a shift in how work is performed, from doing administrative tasks to performing more problem-solving and decision-making. This is the creation of the knowledge worker, where a higher level of cognitive abilities and new behaviors are needed. As a result, the individuals that filled the old job roles may no longer be a good fit.

The organization has just went through a large-scale change initiative where new software applications were installed providing the organization many new capabilities. The data no longer resided in Excel Spreadsheets on individual desktops; now it was consolidated into one centralized database. Applications were now integrated allowing information to flow from one system to the next without having to wait overnight for batch processing, or launching different programs. Most of the administrative tasks such as entering information, navigating to various screens, or printing documents to mail were now performed automatically. The workflow was even automated, eliminating the need to assign work manually to other employees and having it sit in their in-basket waiting action. Work triggers made it possible to reassign the task automatically to other people if there was no action taken within a defined timeframe. Most importantly, employees were empowered to make more decisions without having to involve supervisors and managers. The increased functionality eliminated many of the manual tasks that once consumed many hours of an employee's work day.

Reports were replaced with analytic tools, dashboards, and on-screen indicators. Users of the system had the ability to create their own ad-hoc reports if needed, but the warning flags and dashboard indicators allowed employees to monitor their work in near-real-time and make quick decisions when needed.

During the large-scale change initiative, the business processes were mapped and documented. Starting at the value-chain where the very high levels show how work flows through the major components of the business, down to activities and tasks were defined. Non-system related changes were made to reduce the complexity while improving the overall efficiency. Non-value added tasks were either eliminated or redefined. For the first time, performance metrics were defined for each process. Measurements were defined and taken to determine areas for performance improvement. These metrics were linked to the Key Performance Indicators that were defined in the Balanced Scorecard.

With all of these technological and business process changes, the roles and competency levels had to change. Rather than turning to training to provide the answer, the leadership team needed to examine each position that was impacted by the change, then determine if the employees fit the new job requirements. In order to better understand how the job fit works, we must first understand how jobs are defined.

Job Families are groupings of jobs with similar functions, roles, or skills. All staff jobs are assigned to a job family during the classification process based on the general roles, functions, and skills needed for that particular job.

Each job family consists of different levels or **job classifications**. Once the appropriate job family has been selected, the job classification is determined based on the duties performed, scope of responsibility, level of skill, education requirements, and the potential impact the position has on the business operations.

Positions are a subset of a job classification. A position is based on the job family and classification to determine the appropriate group and level but requires specific and unique set of knowledge, skills, abilities, and behaviors to perform their duties adequately. A project manager job may require a certificate along with a defined length of experience. However, not all project manager jobs are equal. Some positions may have to deal with technical systems and have knowledge of the agile methodology, whereas another project manager position may require a strong understanding of finance, and be involved in managing the project budget. Each position requires a core knowledge of project management, but each requires a different skill set. The ability to work in a unique environment may be a factor as well as having the right behaviors that are needed to perform the tasks to the desired level of performance.

During the transformation initiative, many of the administrative tasks were automated. The integration of systems allowed data to flow seamlessly from one database to the other. The workflow was triggered by specific actions and would automatically reassign the task if no actions were taken in a timely manner. The dashboard provided the employee with a near real-time performance that would flag the user if the process times were reaching their performance limits. The new analytic tools allowed the user to diagnose key performance indicators and service level agreements to make informed decisions just in time.

The competencies for each position should be identified and defined to meet the new requirements defined by the transformation. Once categorized, the competencies for each candidate should be evaluated and compared to the position. Those individuals who most closely match the position competencies should be considered. Although not every individual will match the position exactly. Training can be provided to close the skills gap. However, training will not address the behavioral fit and, therefore, those individual that do not have the right behaviors should not be considered to fill the position. When there is a miss-match of behaviors between the individual and the job role they are fulfilling, the individual may not meet the needs required for the position. The individual will often become frustrated, stressed, and develop negative behaviors. As a result, these negative behaviors can affect the attitudes of other employees creating an unhealthy work environment.

63

Not Your Typical Communication

"Truthful words are not beautiful; beautiful words are not truthful. Good words are not persuasive; persuasive words are not good."

— Lao Tzu

In a recent study quoted in the New York Times stated that individuals receive on average 3,000 messages per day. We get bombarded by emails, text messages, phone calls, IM, web pages, radio, television, newspaper, and the list goes on. Our brains are incapable of processing this amount of information and, as a result, will tune out messages that may not directly impact our life.

At work, we selectively attempt to attend to a few activities while ignoring other distractions, although our attention can be distracted by something else, like the telephone ringing, an instant message, or someone using our name. When we look at our email box, we have a tendency to look to see who sent the message and skim subject lines to determine if the topic pertains to our work or personal lives. Many of these messages are informational that do not require any action. All of these messages become noise that can become a distraction.

Organizational change management communication is different from the ordinary method of target specific or informational communication that inundates most of the messages we receive. For a change to occur, it requires action. We want people to change their current behaviors to new behaviors that are aligned to and support the change vision.

First, let me define organizational change management communication. Many business leaders make the assumption that if they send out a letter, email or even conduct a meeting announcing the new change initiative that they did their part in communicating. Change communication is not a directive, edict, or an announcement. Change communication is the continuous exchange of information to create a vision for the future and explain how the planned change will take them along this new journey. Using a cascading approach to inform and educate leaders from the top, down to the lowest levels should be used to inspire, coach, and instruct how employees should behave differently using new roles, reporting relationships, processes, and tools to achieve the desired result.

The desired state should be both meaningful and achievable to everyone in the organization. The change communication should also describe what the end state will look like when they arrive. This means that the new behaviors are measured and rewarded, while old, undesired behaviors are no longer recognized, even though they once were rewarded.

Behavior Change Communication is different from the ordinary instructional method of communication and is target specific. An organization consists of many sub-groups. The strategy for Behavior Change Communication will vary from group to group. The following points are important in considering the Behavior Change Communication strategy.

- Vulnerability or risk factors of the target audience.
- Any potential conflicts and obstacles in the way to desired change in Behavior.

- Type of message and communication media which can best be used to reach the target audience.
- Type of resources available and assessment of existing knowledge of the target audience about the issue which is going to be addressed.
- The level of respect that the message sender has among the target audience.

There can be several more points in this list, but these are a summary of the key points I feel are important. A successful Behavior Change Communication requires lots of research and meticulous planning about the knowledge content of the topic, along with the behaviors and attitudes of the target audience. This will determine the most effective way to deliver the message and the appropriate timing of the message.

Business units, departments, and workgroups have their own cultures. This is often based on the type of work they perform, the leadership and managerial styles, geographic location, and many other factors. The difference in cultures will influence the method and quality of communication. The language of a financial management specialist is very different from an information technology specialist. The use of slang terms or the interpretation of the meaning of some words can become barriers. Other issues that influence the communication is the prevailing culture, or behavioral norms and expectations. Some examples include: upward and downward communication between staff and management. The indicators that can be measured include: Being forthright or censored; frequent or infrequent; formal or informal; honest or filtered; positive or negative; and acted upon or ignored. Another indicator is the quality of the communication within the specific area. The indicators that can be measured include: timely or delayed; complete or sketchy; straight from the source or through multiple channels, and easily processed or complicated.

Understanding the cultural differences will indicate how effective the communication will be within each area. If we know that the downward communication in a particular area is an issue, then we may choose to deliver the message directly to the employee by allowing them to participate in an organizational wide assembly, or participate in a conference call. Whereas another area may have an issue with upward communication. In this case, the change leader may choose to conduct one-on-one interviews or small group discussions. Using multiple vehicles to communicate change is desired to obtain an exchange of information. Using different people to present the information, and understanding the particular needs of the target audience is critical to ensure effective change communication that will change the behaviors achieving the desired results. Conducting behavior communication is not the act but rather achieving the desired results. Marketing professionals use the rule of 7s, which is delivering the message seven times, using seven different ways. Although this is a guideline, it is the end result, achieving the new behavior that we desire.

64

PROMOTING ORGANIZATIONAL LEARNING

*"An organization's ability to learn, and translate that learning
into action rapidly is the ultimate competitive advantage."*

JACK WELCH

H OW DOES AN organization learn from its accomplishments and mistakes? The big marketing campaign that kicked off last year was a
great success, far exceeding the goal from prior years. The software upgrade
of the enterprise finance system failed twice before, and now the business
is attempting the project for a third time in a row. What was learned that
made the marketing campaign a success, and why did they not learn from
the mistakes from the software upgrade project? Some managers would cite
the unique nature of the project while others would point to the knowledge
and experience of staff members. Although both responses would be correct,
it does not adequately answer the question of how an organization learns.
The success or failure of initiatives cannot be based on chance or the reliance

on key individuals. An organization must develop a process for learning and sharing that information across all areas to continue to be successful and grow.

To achieve and sustain success, several conditions must be met. First, there must be a knowledge management framework that consists of a knowledge development plan, knowledge acquisition approach, and a mechanism for knowledge deployment. The primary goal of knowledge management is to improve organizational performance by enabling individuals to capture, share, and apply their collective knowledge to make optimal decisions in real time. The management of knowledge must go beyond an individual or a localized group of people but extend to the entire organization. Knowledge management and organizational learning are related. The management of knowledge includes the creation and sharing of knowledge, which is consistent with learning. However, learning also involves the decision to change future actions which are typically considered an outcome of knowledge management.

Organizational learning is a set of processes by which organizations not only improve their performance, but can sustain that performance over time. Organizational performance is the outcome of learning where the goals are defined and measured by distinct metrics. However, sustaining a high level of performance requires the organization to anticipate and accept feedback, applying it to existing or new processes. Organizational learning means that an understanding of the interrelationships between processes is constantly evolving and that those relationships themselves are examined and changed as needed.

Knowledge management is inherently collaborative which requires individuals share information. In large organizations where individuals are located several floors or even continents away, collaboration requires technology. The use of collaboration tools can change the way in which people work together. Email, instant messaging, video conferencing, and cloud computing are just a few examples of applications that are used to bridge the distance between employees. However, there are limitations that prevent communication to be as effective as it could. Research shows that 93% of all communication is non-verbal. Therefore, emails, IM's and other messaging services cannot show the inflection in the tone of speech, or the body language that accompanies an answer.

Social networks are another way to think about the role of technology in organizational learning by connecting people together with similar interests. Social networks link people with similar interests together to a new kind of relationship. The more formal roles of employee, customer, boss, vendor, supplier, etc. are replaced by informal, friendly connections. Social networks are a critical resource in building teams and exchanging knowledge in an organization. Knowledge networks can be defined as a special care of social networks in which the links of the network represent shared or related knowledge. If social networks represent who knows who, then knowledge networks represent who knows what. New procedures and practices may be required by management to allow the free exchange of information without the fear of violating confidentiality agreements, proprietary intellectual capital, trade secrets, or business strategies.

Technology and social networks will fail to be effective organizational learning tools if the organization's culture does not support adaptive and constructive behaviors. Because learning implies that past performance needs to be improved, and organization must be willing to admit to changing circumstances, less than optimal past performance or some other level of failure. Bureaucratic, oppositional, or controlling behavioral styles may become barriers to the adoption of new technologies and the use of social networks to adopt and support organizational learning.

Bureaucratic behaviors within an organization are generally defined by an abundance of rules that dictate how employees perform their work and interact with others. Jobs and reporting relationships are well defined and enforced. Individuals back up those with the most authority, to avoid confrontations and be accepted by others. In an effort to avoid risks, employees are reluctant to present new ideas that may challenge the status quo. Since employees are aware of their scope of authority within their role, they will not share information at the risk of confrontation. Learning is limited to the chosen few individuals while the rest of the organization follows standards and accepted practices.

Oppositional and Defiant behaviors within an organization are supported by managers who use strict controls to quickly identify errors made by employees, so punishment and blame can be issued. Employees are encouraged to monitor their work and look for mistakes since the focus is on individual performance. Learning is non-existent due to the defiant nature of employees. Those that have knowledge do not share due to fear of losing power or control. This group rejects conformity and, therefore, will challenge standards. They can lack involvement and commitment especially in times of change. With this attitude, employees do not participate in learning activities.

Influencing and Controlling behaviors use individual power bases to pit individuals and groups against each other. Many senior leaders will promote healthy competition. However, this creates winners and losers, creating a divide within the organization. Competition is good only when everyone on the team pulls together. There is a tendency to have tribal knowledge within these organizations. Since the information is power, learning is confined to individuals or small groups. In keeping this bit of knowledge to themselves, they may be able to use this to outperform or out whit others to look good in front of their superiors.

Adaptive and Constructive behaviors within an organization are formed when individuals work together and support each other to achieve a common, realistic goal. Individuals work to enrich themselves with knowledge and share what they have learned with others. Mistakes are viewed as learning events. Individuals are encouraged to try new things, to have stretch goals, and to help other co-works to achieve a common goal. This is the environment where organizational learning fosters and grows.

65

TEAM SIZE MATTERS

"The way a team plays as a whole determines its success. You may have the greatest bunch of individual stars in the world, but if they don't play together, the club won't be worth a dime."

— BABE RUTH

CAN A PROJECT get completed quicker with more people assigned? Is there greater efficiency and a higher level of quality attained when more people are assigned to the project? These are questions that can haunt a project manager. Although deciding on the size of a team is part art and part science. However, science is now providing us some good information that can aid in our planning.

The consensus among social researchers agrees that a large team can be unmanageable and ineffective to meet defined objectives. Smaller teams are perceived to be much more agile and can effectively deliver results. Most experts would agree that the ideal team size consists of five to ten people. But how did they come to that conclusion?

There has been a considerable amount of research performed on team size and effectiveness in recent years. The indicators that have an adverse impact on team size include geographical separation, the type of task that needs to be performed, and the level of complexity, diversity, and personal work style.

The team size was analyzed in a paper titled, "Team Mental Models and Team Performance" published in the January 2006 edition of the Journal of Organizational Behavior. Each person on the team counts as a valued contributor. When two people work together, they tend to exchange ideas and function effectively. When three people come together there becomes an opportunity to have power battles, two against one. There is a notion that an even number of people may be different from odd numbers for some reason.

When five people join the team, there tends to be diminishing returns on how much individuals will contribute unless they are motivated, or their task assignment is challenging. When a team expands over eight or nine people, it becomes cumbersome to manage, and there is a tendency for the team to break into sub-groups. Depending upon the group's task that would have either a positive or negative effect. As the team grows larger, there is a tendency for "social loafing: where a team member will not contribute at their desired level. This diminished lack of contribution occurs when the individual is not recognized for their knowledge, perspective and contribution. Teams can operate as a social unit; members will self-govern themselves especially when the tasks become more complex. Larger teams lose the quality relationships with one another and, as a result, will decrease individual performance due to the intra-team process and support.

The research also examined the value of diversity and found some interesting results. The diversity represented by gender, race, culture and age led to conflict and poor social interaction. They found that people who are similar to themselves and share similar mental models have greater cohesion and can anticipate each other's responses and coordinate effectively when time is of the essence and opportunities for overt communication and debate are limited. However, when team members are similar to others but have differing viewpoints, some members can become upset and can raise the level of conflict on the team. That in itself is not a bad thing unless the conflict gets in the way of being able to think through a problem and do what needs to be done. Teams with greater diversity can bring different perspectives and insights, but will take the team longer to develop new mental models and will slow the progress of task completion.

Emotional stability is one of the most important and powerful predictors of team effectiveness. When team members become easily agitated, worry a lot and has a strong temper, it is bad for the team. A single team member can diminish the energy and de-motivate the entire team. Within an organization, individual teams can compete against each other which can create a win-lose environment that will diminish the overall performance and efficiency.

Virtual teams tend to be less effective than those that can interact face-to-face when it comes to innovation. This cannot be said for productivity since virtual team members can work independently to complete an assigned task on schedule. Teams that rely on electronic communication are less successful than those that understand why communication in person is important. Email is a terrible medium since it does not relate emotion very well and can lead to a misunderstanding. Since 93% of communication is non-verbal, the ability to effectively communicate something very important requires face-to-face interaction to work effectively together.

While teams are hard to create, they are also hard to fix when they don't function properly. Therefore, to improve the effectiveness of a team, the following steps should be taken:

- Ensure that the team is clear about its goal
- Assign the right members to tasks they are capable of performing
- Each team member should have a clear focus as to their role and task
- Strong leadership is needed to direct the team, remove barriers and define the structure and process

The above compilation broadly outlines various perspectives pertaining to team size. It gives some direction on how to view team size in different business situations. However, the critical factor to keep in mind is the importance of justifying the presence of each and every member of the team. The key deciders should be the individual roles, the complexity of the task and the need for a certain number of people to execute the job effectively. Overall, research does seem to indicate that ultimately, small is the better way to go when forming a team.

66

THE GOAL OF ORGANIZATIONAL CHANGE MANAGEMENT

"One's philosophy is not the best expressed in words; it is expressed in the choices one makes. In the long run, we shape our lives, and we shape ourselves. The process never ends until we die. And, the choices we make are ultimately our own responsibility."

— ELEANOR ROOSEVELT

ORGANIZATIONAL CHANGE MANAGEMENT has now become a part of most business transformation initiatives to ensure that employees are aware of the changes taking place and that the change is sustainable once the initiative gets implemented. Many of the business transformation initiatives are centered on the implementation of new software applications that impact a major portion of the business such as finance and accounting, supply chain management, Payroll and benefits management, warehousing and so forth.

Businesses commit a great deal of time and money to ensure that these applications get implemented with minimal disruption to the business, as quickly as possible and provide the capabilities as promised. The senior leadership knows that the business does not have the expertise or staff to undertake such a project, nor do they want to take on the risk to the business if the implementation does not meet the expected requirements. Consulting firms are contracted to supply the required staff with the knowledge and experience in implementation, and to assume a large portion of the risk. Due to the nature of the project, a great deal of resources and attention is placed on the technical side of the project with organizational change management responsible for preparing the organization for the inevitable change.

With much of the attention placed on the technology, it is easy for many of the senior leaders to set the project's goal of a software implementation, rather than solving the business issue. This shift in project goals will have a huge impact on organizational change management. When the focus is only on installing software, the expectation of the employees is to accept the change and be capable of using it when the time comes. Therefore, the organizational change management activities will be relegated to communication and training. This solution may appear to be acceptable since the software will provide new functionality, and the employees will be adequately trained. However, did this solution solve the original business problem? In many cases, the new software may have provided new capabilities and functionality that was not available in the old system but did not address the underlying problem which requires changes in behavior. Likewise, the project, although quite large should not be considered "transformative". Business Transformation is defined as a complete change in the way in which business is performed. In addition to technical changes, it requires changes in business processes, the organizational reporting relationships, and new behaviors. What many project leaders have not fully realized is that changes in technical systems such as new software applications will change the service levels (time) and the performance indicators (quality). These are some of the new behaviors that will require attention.

The goal of organizational change management in a business transformation initiative is twofold: the initial focus is to raise awareness of the change vision and to generate a sense of urgency and excitement among employees to build support in order to accept and embrace the change. During this phase, the OCM practitioner creates a climate where senior leadership and staff employees understand the business problem and how it is hurting the business. The vision for change is defined and communicated by the senior leadership that will not only tell people what will change, but how the organization will look and feel when the change is complete. The transformation initiative becomes a high priority as the leadership creates excitement about the change that will occur. The change management activities focus on changing attitudes of individuals, but it cannot be sustained over a long period of time.

Once the organization understands the business problem and accepts the change, attention shifts to understanding what new behaviors or actions are needed to sustain the change. There could be many reasons why new behaviors are needed: information may not be shared resulting in timely delays; employees may be frustrated resulting in high turnover; the business process may be excessively complex or require a number of approvals that affect the quality or performance; and the new functionality within the software may force some employees to perform actions such as approvals that are not normally performed at that level.

The required behaviors needed to support the change should also align with the organization's core values. If the organization does not value the change, it will not be sustainable. If putting people first is a core value and the change promotes making more sales at whatever cost, then that change is not sustainable. An example of this type of behavior would be to establish competition between two business units: one will win, and the other will lose, rather than working together to accomplish their sales goal.

The outcome of the organizational change management activities applies to any organization undergoing a business transformation. These outcomes include:

- The ability to be continually innovative and adapt to change quickly and effectively
- To have an effectively problem-solving and make quality decisions in a timely manner
- Increase customer and employee satisfaction
- To provide quality services and produce quality products

Each outcome can be measured and tied to specific drivers of behavior. These drivers can be used as levers for change. There are a variety of behavioral drivers that can be identified and measured that affect the stated outcomes. An organization that is very hierarchical, for example, can limit what an individual employee can do to solve a problem, or satisfy a customer. Information that is not viewed as timely, complete, or credible from a supervisor will create uncertainty and stress among staff employees. Restricting access to system information may limit one's ability to formulate an accurate decision. Drivers that can create unwanted behaviors may be unique to a business unit, department, or functional area. Therefore, assessments should include demographic data to identify patterns of behavior.

67

BEHAVIORS THAT FIT THE JOB

"If A equals success, then the formula is A equals X plus Y and Z, with X being work, Y play, and Z is keeping your mouth shut."

— ALBERT EINSTEIN

ONE OF THE challenges that people in a complex, rapidly changing workplace face is the need to fulfill many different roles in their work. Each role may have a different set of expectations, not only in terms of 'what' we do, but also, in terms of 'how' we do it. Expectations can change considerably from one role to another. We often form certain expectations of behavior around certain roles and are quite shocked when those expectations do not match reality. When we think of a judge, we may picture in our mind an older gentleman in black robes acting very reserved and stoic. When we observe the judge acting differently by laughing out loud, telling jokes, and being very animated, we may not take their direction seriously since they do not conform to our predefined model. We also perceive our own roles in a certain way and then act accordingly. You may have just been promoted to a manager position and believe that managers stay detached and hard to approach. As a result, you may act that way because you believe that type of behavior is expected.

Behaviors that may be very effective in one role may be disastrous in another role. For example, if we take the behavior that makes us very successful in our job and attempt to use it at home, we may not be effective at all. Or, if we use behavior that is effective in the role of a parent with small children with our peers at work, we may experience conflict and resentment. Using behavior that is effective in the role of a line worker may not work well as a manager or supervisor. Clearly, a process for identifying which behavior would be most effective and appropriate in which role is essential for clarifying and communicating role expectations.

Most people think about the competencies that are required to perform the job. Knowledge, skills, and abilities are defined in a job description. However, a candidate can have very strong competencies but still fail at their role. Each role requires certain behaviors to be effective. I will provide an illustration of a behavioral fit:

A large company was seeking to hire several administrative clerks to fill a variety of roles from the mail room to the receptionist. The company screened several candidates and selected some to proceed to the testing phase. A skills test was administered to the candidates, and those that received high scores were offered the position.

After two months, two of the new clerks were having disciplinary issues. One employee was assigned to the reception desk. Her job was to greet visitors, answer the phone and type letters. She was very task oriented and told visitors to hold while she finished typing the letter. The other employee was assigned to the mail room to deliver mail throughout the building. This employee was very social and took the time to engage in conversations which resulted in delaying the delivery of the mail.

Both employees were placed on probation when the human resource manager recognized the behavioral differences and decided to swap their roles. After two months, the plan to exchange roles was a success. Each employee was happy in their new role and performed well. Even though each employee had strong skills, the behaviors needed for the roles were quite different.

To ensure a successful job fit, a position impact assessment tool was used to identify the required behaviors and the competencies for the position. This establishes a job/ position benchmark that define all of the necessary requirements. The same criteria are then used to match the competencies and behaviors of the individual candidates to the position. Those candidates who most closely match the position benchmark should be the best fit. Candidates who most closely fit the requirements of the position will have greater satisfaction, less job stress, and produce a higher quality of work.

When there is a mismatch of one or more skills competencies between the candidate and the position benchmark, training can be used to close the gap. However, if there is a mismatch in the behaviors, training will not resolve the problem and potential problems may arise. Mismatched behavioral expectations may be displayed as a "poor attitude" or other performance issues. Therefore, a good rule to remember is that "you can train to skills but not behaviors."

A position impact analysis is a tool that provides a process for describing and discussing expectations for role-based skill needs and behaviors for specific jobs. It is designed to collect and process individual perceptions of the behavioral expectations of 'how' a role, function, job or position should be fulfilled for anyone to be effective in that role. A position impact analysis is used to describe a specific role within a defined environment, focusing on how the role needs to be fulfilled, regardless of who is in that role.

When candidates are screened for the job or position based on the required skills only, and there is no consideration as to the personality behaviors of the candidate for that position, the result may be unfulfilled expectations. A position impact analysis can be used to collect employee profile information for a position. Then, a clearly defined set of shared expectations for competencies and behavior in that role can be developed and communicated in a non-threatening manner, reducing potential conflict. The analysis also can be used to anticipate changes in competencies and behavior necessary for a change in an employee's role. The change may result in a career move or a minor change in the process of performing their work. In addition, the position impact analysis can be used to identify the specific differences in behavioral expectations from the old role to the new role resulting in improved team development, problem-solving, and customer service expectations. To ensure a successful business transformation, it is highly recommended to assess the new behaviors in each job role that are needed for the change.

68

The CEO's Role in Business Transformation

*"Public hangings are teaching moments. Every company has to
do it. A teaching moment is worth a thousand CEO speeches.
CEOs can talk and blab each day about culture, but the employees all know who the jerks are. They could name the jerks
for you. It's just cultural. People just don't want to do it."*

— Jack Welch

In today's business environment, companies cannot settle for incremental
improvement; they must periodically undergo performance transformations to get, and stay, on top. But in the volumes of pages on how to go about
implementing a transformation, surprisingly little addresses the role of one
important person. What exactly should the CEO be doing, and how different
is this role from that of the executive team or the initiative's sponsors?

As diverse as the type of organizations, there is no single model for success. Moreover, the exact nature of the CEO's role will be influenced by the magnitude, urgency, and nature of the transformation; the capabilities and failings of the organization; and the personal style of the leader.

Despite these variations, our experience with scores of major transformation efforts, combined with research we have undertaken over the past decade, suggests that four key functions collectively define a successful role for the CEO in a transformation:

1. Making the transformation meaningful. People will go to extraordinary lengths for causes they believe in, and a powerful transformation story will create and reinforce their commitment. The ultimate impact of the story depends on the CEO's willingness to make the transformation personal, to engage others openly, and to spotlight successes as they emerge.

2. Role-modeling desired mindsets and behavior. Successful CEOs typically embark on their own personal transformation journey. Their actions encourage employees to support and practice the new types of behavior.

3. Building a strong and committed top team. To harness the transformative power of the top team, CEOs must make tough decisions about who has the ability and motivation to make the journey.

4. Relentlessly pursuing impact. There is no substitute for CEOs rolling up their sleeves and getting personally involved when significant financial and symbolic value is at stake.

Everyone has a role to play in a performance transformation. The role of CEOs is unique in that they stand at the top of the pyramid and all the other members of the organization take cues from them. CEOs who give only lip service to a transformation will find everyone else doing the same. Those who fail to model the desired mindsets and behavior or who opt out of vital initiatives risk seeing the transformation lose focus. Only the boss of all bosses can ensure that the right people spend the right amount of time driving the necessary changes.

Transformations require extraordinary energy: employees must fundamentally rethink and reshape the business while continuing to run it day to day. Where does this energy come from? A powerful transformation story helps employees believe in the effort by answering their big questions, which can range from how the transformation will affect the company down to how it will affect them. The story's ultimate impact will depend on not just having compelling answers to these questions but also the CEO's willingness and ability to make things personal, to engage others openly, and to spotlight successes as they emerge.

Adopt a personal approach: CEOs who take the time to personalize the story of the transformation can unlock significantly more energy for it than those who dutifully present the PowerPoint slides that their working teams created for them. Personalizing the story forces CEOs to consider and share with others the answers to such questions as "Why are we changing?"; "How will we get there?" and "How does this relate to me?"

Actions speak louder than words. It is one thing to tell a compelling story to get people to embrace the message, it is very different for them to take action, this is the role of the leader. Everyone looks toward the leader to "walk the talk" and take action to show that the story is more than mere words. If the transformation requires cost-cutting measures, then the CEO must show by example, cutting back on expenses. Stop taking frequent trips, or even making the appearance of elaborate spending. Overall, the best way to be a role model is not to change one or two things, but to establish personal standards that are high, then the CEO can rightfully demand the same of the rest of the organization.

Transformation initiatives can create hardships within the organization. Changes disrupt the normal routine and can create stress among some and may motivate others. The CEO should make it part of their responsibility to know how subordinate leaders and staff will react to different situations. Knowing how the employees will react to changes will help in deciding the best way to employ the staff to achieve effective results. Assigning tasks and delegating authority to support the transformation promotes mutual confidence and respect between the CEO and the team.

The CEO's involvement must be more than making a presence at meetings, or walking around checking on the status of activities. Before the CEO can expect the employees to perform, they need to know what is expected of them. The CEO must communicate instructions in a clear, concise manner, and allow the employees a chance to ask questions. The CEO should personally check on the progress periodically to confirm the assigned tasks are properly accomplished. Barriers that prevent tasks to be completed on time should be identified and removed. A rapid estimate of the situation and making sound decisions based on the situation is the best way for the CEO to be actively involved. Employees respect a leader who is responsive to the needs of others.

69

MANAGING TRUST

"Set your expectations high; find men and women whose integrity and values you respect; get their agreement on a course of action; and give them your ultimate trust."

JOHN FELLOWS AKERS

TRANSFORMING A BUSINESS requires a great deal of trust from many people. The Board of Directors places trust in the Chief Executive Officer to fundamentally change the business operation to meet strategic goals. Turning the responsibility over to a subordinate leader to guide the initiative takes trust. Trust is also required in the consulting firms that support the initiative, the software vendors, the employees who rely on the company to provide a paycheck, and even the customers who rely on the products and services that the organization provides.

Our definition of trust is simple: It is both character (who you are) and competence (your strengths and the results you produce). Trust is the enabling power of leadership influence. It is not soft, slow, risky, or easy. It is a measurable, definable component of all leadership success. It can be both taught and learned.

The proof of the value of trust in a business transformation is compelling: "Organizations with high trust outperform organizations with low trust by nearly three times." (Watson Wyatt 2002).

Here are some myths and realities that people have about trust:

Myth	Reality
Trust is a soft measure	Trust is hard, real, and quantifiable. It measurably affects both the speed of change and the associated cost.
Trust is slow to develop	Nothing is as fast as the speed of trust.
Trust is built solely on integrity	Trust is a function of character (which includes integrity) and competence.
Once lost, trust cannot be restored	Though difficult, in most cases lost trust can be restored.
You can't teach trust	Trust can be effectively taught and learned, and it can become leverageable, a strategic advantage
Trusting people is too risky.	Not trusting people is a greater risk
You establish trust one person at a time	Establishing trust with one establishes trust in many.

Trust in the old economy was the natural outcome of a select few, great organizations. Today, it is the price of entry into the new, global economy. In today's world, you are not only competing with others in your state, but also on your continent and the five other civilized continents on the planet. You are negotiating in cultures in which trust is non-negotiable.

Trust enters into so many facets of business transformation that at times it can make your brain hurt. Trust is the heart of most change management initiatives. If employees don't trust the proposed changes you are negotiating, chances are, you will take extra steps to limit your risk exposure. These extra risk insurance steps can actually get in the way of exposing great change opportunities for improvement. Conversely, if we are open to trusting the management or staff we are negotiating change with the possibility of collaboration gets brighter. Both parties may positively nudge each to take a greater positive risk in cementing new accretive agreements benefiting both parties.

Here are five tips to build trust in business negotiations: Remember... trusted people get more deals done!

1. **Listen to stakeholders-** If you want to build trust with a change management partner, you have to treat them as a unique person. Everyone has objectives, goals, and aspirations. We have angst. We all have a story. We have worries. Bills to pay. And, most importantly loved ones to care for. If we thoughtfully listen to the management and staff and ask the right questions a common understanding will be gained.

2. **Succeed with Deeds-** Trust doesn't just happen. Someone has to start to build a foundation of trust. Someone has to take a positive risk and initiate the trust process. Take the leap of faith. Be the change champion who says... "Here is something we value that I know will enhance our discussions around change."

3. **Creative Solutions-** Sharing creative ideas is definitely a way to build trust. Think in terms of mutually exclusive and collectively exhaustive to create new ideas that will make your organization unique while meeting the needs of the employees, the business, customers, suppliers, and the community.

4. **Offer Value-** In a "Seller's Market" we used to say "Build it, and they will come." The problem with this thinking is that we have been in a "Buyer's Market" for many years, and those who are buying want two dollars of value for every dollar they spend. This puts extra pressure on our point of difference and our value equation. If you offer true value.... they will trust you more!

5. **Show Up-** We trust actions and personal integrity not posters on walls with catchy phrases. Our personal brand is actually a summation of our reliable, positive, repeatable promises. When business leaders ask employees to become engaged and actively involved in the change process, they are asking if there is trust. If there is the slightest bit of hesitation, the leader should ask for an explanation. Trust is owed to no one. Trust is earned. Trust cannot be expected. Trust is given in good faith.

In many organizations, trust is one of their core values that they espouse. An adaptive and constructive organizational culture supports trust in every aspect of their work: in the way Employees are selected and placed within the organization, in the way the team functions, the way jobs are designed, and many more drivers of behavior.

70

Making Change
Communication Work

*"Effective communication is 20% what you know and 80%
how you feel about what you know."*

— Jim Rohn

The advancement of technology has made it much easier to communicate now compared to just a few years ago. Smartphones are no longer telephones with added features, but rather communication devices where texting and Snapchat are used more than the traditional telephone call. There are many messages that are being sent, but how do we figure out what is important? How do we navigate through all this information to make decisions that lead to success? We need to be able to filter through all the noise and piece strings of information together to make effective decisions. Eighty percent of our communication efforts and content are ineffective when measured by the impact it has on people's decisions to change their behaviors. This relates to a very low return on investment from our efforts to drive change.

The goal of change communication is to provide people what they need to make informed choices about whether and how to comply with or commit to the change. The communication needs to build trust with candid information about the need for and the difficulty of changing, including the consequences of not changing. Then, to report the progress or lack of progress, to that the people can be responsible contributors to the change.

There are basically two types of communication messages: Key messages and behavioral communication. Key messages communication is the delivery of any information that does not require action. Any communication for which there is no discernible consequence if the recipient ignores the message. Behavioral communication, on the other hand, is the delivery of any information, in any form or format, which is designed to drive a specific action with clearly defined measures, consequences, tools, and rewards.

Change leaders make an assumption of the focus of the typical transformation message.

- 80%   Why we are changing
- 10%   Overall organizational priorities
- 10%   What's in it for us?

However, stakeholders require a different focus in order to change their behaviors.

- 10%   Why we are changing
- 10%   Overall organizational priorities
- 20%   How the employees will be measured and the consequences
- 50%   The tools and support provided to make the change
- 10%   What's in it for us?

To change behaviors, employees need the answers to just five questions:

1. Why change? How is this important to what I do?
2. What do you want me to do differently, and what are the priorities?

3. How will I be measured and what are the consequences?
4. What tools and support do I get to help me make this change?
5. What's in it for me? How will this change benefit what I do?

Most of what passes for change communication is based on a partial premise. Knowing why we are changing, where we are heading, or even creating a shared vision are just steps in the negotiation process. Change communication is about renegotiating the relationship between the organization, the individual, and the customer.

The delivery of any information that changes what is important: Organizing and delivering what we know about what is important, redefining rules and roles, and how we will work in the future gives the employee the ability to navigate through change for themselves. Executive sponsors of change can no longer manage messages and delivery vehicles, promoting the illusion of control. This form of communication is mostly key messages. The executive sponsor must organize and deliver information about what is known in a way that gives others the ability to navigate through change for themselves and form their own conclusions.

The key activities within the change communication strategy ensure that the behavioral communication is obtained. Stakeholders should be segmented into groups and assess the potential impact of the change, creating audiences. Then, a communication audit should be performed to determine the quality and methods of communication. Once analyzed, a change communication plan should be developed for each phase of the initiative since different demands are placed on the stakeholders. When creating a communication plan, include detailed components such as: the objective of the message, the desired outcome, the person delivering the message, the frequency and timing of the message, and the vehicle used to deliver the message.

A research study revealed that when a company president sends a message down through the organization the level of understanding of the message decreases.

- Vice-Presidents 67%
- Directors   56%

- Line Managers 40%
- Supervisors   30%
- Employees   20%

With this dramatic level of misunderstanding, messages must be sent multiple times using a variety of communication vehicles. It is important to remember that there are three parts to effective communication: the sender, the message, and the receiver. The sender and receiver must share an area of commonality to ensure that the process of exchanging ideas is complete once the receiver understands the sender's message.

71

STRUCTURING YOUR ORGANIZATION TO ENHANCE PERFORMANCE

"Every company has two organizational structures: The formal one is written on the charts; the other is the everyday relationships of the men and women in the organization."

— HAROLD S. GENEEN

Organizations are established to meet a need to provide specific goods or services. Organizational structures can take many forms. These are influenced by factors such as its purpose, size, and the complexity of the tasks it performs, the external environment, and its culture. Its products, services or where it is located, also determine which structure is best. The structure chosen will govern the way in which the organization operates and can have positive and negative effects. Traditional bureaucratic organizations such as those found in federal and state agencies have a very hierarchical structure. This has many layers and a long chain of command from the top to the bottom layer. In the twentieth century, as organizations grew, hierarchical organizations were popular. This type of tall structure ensured effective command of the organization because of the narrow span of control. (This is the number of people who report to a manager or supervisor).

In contrast to a hierarchical structure is the flat organizational structure. This structure has fewer layers or sometimes just one layer of management. This means that the chain of command from the top to the bottom of the organization is short, and the span of control is wide. With fewer layers for information to be cascaded down communication channels are clear and effective. Another alternative is a matrix structure. This type of structure is commonly used for project based work within an organization. The team is made up of individuals with specialist skills, such as software architecture, network administrators, business analysts, and other specialists, who all get their work assignments under a project manager and administratively report to their own functional manager.

But what does the organizational structure have to do with meeting or exceeding operational performance standards such as customer and employee satisfaction, and quality services and products? The type of structure an organization assumes is greatly influenced by the type of work that they business is engaged. When an organization does business in a highly regulated industry such as pharmaceuticals, nuclear power, or capital markets, the organization will take on the same type of controls in assigning roles to control their employees as what it does in controlling its products and services.

Core values are those traits of behaviors that are encouraged and supported by management. An example of core values may include a trust, teamwork, and creativity. In order to promote these core values, the organizational structure must be designed to support those behaviors. A hierarchical structure with multiple layers of approval is designed to limit collaboration and, therefore, is not conducive to support teamwork. Within a hierarchical structure, jobs are often narrowly defined resulting in a lack of trust to make decisions at their level of authority. Creativity is also diminished when there is an abundance of rules and layers of control where a good idea can often be stifled by others within the chain of command.

Matrix organizations are equally as bad in supporting core values in achieving the desired outcomes of performance. Effectiveness decreases when an employee reports to two different bosses, each with their own agenda, each with their own needs, and an employee who is unable to satisfy the needs of either boss.

Flat organizational structures offer great autonomy, variety, and significance in job design. Flat organizations are defined by few management layers with a wider span of authority. When implemented correctly, this structure leads to faster decisions, satisfied customers, and happier employees. Incorrectly used, however, flat organizations can be magnets for job confusion and decreased customer loyalty. Flat organizations promote teamwork. Workplace Teams can be formal in that people are brought together by different functions or departments to work on a specific project. There are also informal teams in the workplace, for example; a team that is working together to organize a social event. However, individuals can also be part of a formal or informal team outside of work. A football team is an example of a formal team. It has a team captain with the rest of the team having specific positions or roles for the purpose of scoring or preventing goals. Informal teams could be a group of friends who meet outside of school or college who share a common interest such as cycling. A team is more than a group of people who happen to work together. An effective team is one which:

- Shares a common purpose
- Respects and supports each other
- Has high commitment to achieving targets
- Has a clear understanding of the work and the role of each team member
- Is good at generating and sharing ideas
- Has open communication between team members

The sharing, respect, and commitment among team members is needed to create an adaptive and constructive organizational culture that produces outcomes such as innovation and adaptability to change; efficient problem-solving and quality decision-making; improved customer and employee satisfaction; and a higher quality of products and services. These outcomes of behaviors often align and support the organization's core values.

72

FITTING A JOB LIKE A PAIR OF SHOES

*"You cannot tailor-make the situations in life, but you can
tailor-make the attitudes to fit those situations."*

— ZIG ZIGLAR

WHEN WE NEED a new pair of shoes, we have the opportunity to look
at all of the different types and styles that are available. We narrow
down the choices based on how we are going to use them: at work, at play, or
maybe based on the season. The next decision point is the price of the shoe;
is it within our budget. Now the decision comes down to fit and style. We
are able to try on the shoes at the store and walk around to test if they are too
snug in the toes, if the soles are too slick, or if they are comfortable. Finally,
we look at the shoe for the style; this is purely a judgment call based on our
particular taste. While the shoes that were chosen may all fit the criteria in
terms of use, budget, fit and style, the final decision is based upon emotion,
or how we feel when wearing the shoe. The same can be said for the type of
job we choose.

When we are seeking a job, we often learn about the position from a job description that is posted on the internet or newspaper. We filter our decision to apply based upon job title, and the short description of duties that are listed. If we are lucky, the name of the company along with the address is somewhere in the ad. We then make the decision if the company is located within a reasonable commute time from our home. We may even evaluate the company to determine if it is a place where we could feel comfortable working. Once we have determined if the job description and company fit our expectations, we move forward submitting our resume to the hiring manager or human resources recruiter for review.

Scanning through hundreds of resumes, by chance something, catches their interest. It may have been your previous employer, a keyword, or phrase, or just the luck of the draw that your resume made it to a shortlist of about 25 for further review. A single phrase that you included on your resume three positions ago elevated your resume to the top, qualifying you for a phone screening interview.

The recruiter sets up a phone call a week later for thirty minutes. When the day finally arrives, you make the first connection. Starting with describing the structure of the call, the recruiter proceeds to describe the company and the position. The next question follows with, so, tell me about yourself. Being well prepared, you give an oral summary of your resume that is already in their hands. If the recruiter is serious about the position, you get scheduled for a face-to-face interview. If not, you know they were just checking off the boxes, so their stats meet the recruiters performance standard of so many resumes screened, so many phone interviews, so many initial interviews and so on.

The face-to-face interview is scheduled the following week. You show up with your best clothes to make a good impression armed with a few copies of your resume. You are ushered into a conference room where the hour long interview starts with an overview of the company along with an overview of the position. Then they ask to provide a quick summary of your background. Then the interviewer asks to describe why you were seeking a new job and to describe why you would want to work for this company. After a few specific questions about various points in your resume, you are asked if you have any questions before escorted to the door.

After a few days, you hear that they want to see you again for a second round of interviews with different people. Things are looking up! The new interview is scheduled in two weeks to accommodate everyone's schedule. You arrive with your best clothes and resumes in hand. You are escorted to the same conference room, not seeing the work areas. In this interview, an employee asks you very specific questions to ascertain your knowledge of your profession in very generic terms. If you didn't hesitate or look lost, you most likely passed that gate. The other employee in the interview asks for your ideas about a situation they are currently facing. With very little context of the situation, you give it your best shot to provide an answer. Running out of time, they ask you if you have any questions as they escort you to the door.

At this point in the interview process, neither the employees nor you have gained a deeper insight into how your skills and personality will be a fit for the position. Finally, you receive an offer from the recruiter. The compensation package meets your needs, and you accept based upon the limited information. You have no idea of the physical work setting other than the glimpse of what you saw in the interview. You do not know how your coworkers interact with each other. You don't even know what to expect in terms of work performance standards.

Many of us were introduced to companies and jobs where a job fit is questionable. Many managers believe that if you appear to have all the skills, experience, and a good personality then you would have a good match. The truth is that to ensure a good job fit requires a behavioral fit between the candidate and the company. Skills can be taught and developed over time whereas behaviors are part of your personal makeup. Behavioral matching starts with sharing the same core values and beliefs. To ensure a good job match starts by defining behaviors of the position, and then matching against the candidates.

73

USING LEAN TECHNIQUES
IN SERVICE INDUSTRIES

*"I am concerned about any attrition in customer traffic at
Starbucks, but I don't want to use the economy, commodity
prices or consumer confidence as an excuse. We must maintain
a value proposition to our customers as well as differentiate the
Starbucks Experience. That is the key."*

— HOWARD SCHULTZ

M ANY LEADERS OF service related companies are seeking a way to apply
the same lean concepts that manufacturing organizations have been
doing for years and doing it well in their production operations. Pure services companies like banks and insurance companies are just now starting to
explore how Lean concepts can be adapted. In many cases, they're looking
at Lean because they're being asked to do more with the static or declining

headcounts. The core idea is to maximize customer value while minimizing waste. Simply, lean means creating more value for customers with fewer resources.

A lean organization understands customer value and focuses its key processes to increase it continuously. The ultimate goal is to provide perfect value to the customer through a perfect value creation process that has zero waste. To accomplish this, lean thinking changes the focus of management from optimizing separate technologies, assets, and vertical departments to optimizing the flow of products and services through entire value streams that flow horizontally across technologies, assets, and departments to customers. Eliminating waste along entire value streams, instead of at isolated points, creates processes that need less human effort, less space, less capital, and less time to make products and services at far less costs and with much fewer defects, compared with traditional business systems. Companies are able to respond to changing customer desires with a high variety, high quality, low cost, and with very fast throughput times. Also, information management becomes much simpler and more accurate.

Concepts of continuous improvement became popular within the United States in the late 1970's when Japan was able to produce high-quality goods at competitive costs. In the early 1980's the Total Quality Management revolution was started using concepts from W. Edwards Deming to combat the economic turmoil that had ensued. It was Deming who taught the Japanese in 1950 how to improve product quality, testing, and sales by various means, including the application of statistical methods. Joseph Juran, a strong proponent of quality management also worked with the Japanese companies at the same time as Deming, although independently. Juran used control charts used at Bell Labs, incorporating the Pareto principle stating that 80% of a problem are caused by 20% of the causes.

The Toyota Motor company incorporated many of Deming's and Juran's principles including quality circles and Shewhart cycle of Plan, Do, Check, Act. The Toyota Production System became the model where methods, techniques, and tools to improve quality and streamline processes. In the late 1980's the term "lean" was coined to describe Toyota's business during the late 1980s by a research team headed by Jim Womack, Ph.D., at MIT's International Motor Vehicle Program.

There is a popular misconception that lean is suited only for manufacturing mainly because of the focus that has been on manufacturing companies. The continuous improvement techniques apply to every business and every process. It is not a tactic or a cost reduction program, but a way of thinking and acting for an entire organization.

However, there are differences in the tools and techniques that fit better in a manufacturing environment than a service organization. I will point out some of the more common differences:

- There is typically greater involvement of customers in the production process. In many cases, the customer is a supplier to the process. Sometimes the involvement is so ingrained in the process that you end up with co-production with the customer

- Since services processes are often very people-centric (vs. machine-centric), it is very difficult to get to real standardization

- Quality is an experience, *not* just a measurement against specifications. The inability to standardize the process makes it very difficult to standardize quality. The customer's definition of quality is a perception, subjective vs. objective

- There is much less visibility to what is happening. Information is flowing, not a product, and that information can be digital, paper or even verbal. And, HOW it flows, often has little or no standardization

- I.T. systems play a much bigger role. They enable the process but can also be a rigid constraint on the process. There may be multiple and often unintegrated systems. Workarounds persist in the form of excel spreadsheets, word documents, etc.

- Work in Progress and inventory are often hidden or ignored, but they are there and can have the same negative impacts as in a manufacturing environment (e.g. wasted resources, longer lead times, more variation

- Womack and Jones, authors of Lean Thinking, recommend that managers and executives that embark on lean transformations think about three fundamental business issues that should guide the transformation of the entire organization:
- Purpose: What customer problems will the enterprise solve to achieve its own purpose of prospering?
- Process: How will the organization assess each major value stream to make sure each step is valuable, capable, available, adequate, flexible, and that all the steps are linked by the flow, pull, and leveling?
- People: How can the organization ensure that every important process has someone responsible for continually evaluating that value stream in terms of business purpose and lean process? How can everyone who touches the value stream be actively engaged in operating it correctly and continually improving it?

"Just as a carpenter needs a vision of what to build in order to get the full benefit of a hammer, Lean Thinkers need a vision before picking up our lean tools," said Womack. "Thinking deeply about the purpose, process, and people is the key to doing this."

74

Ten Key Ways to Adapt to Change

"In any moment of decision, the best thing you can do is the right thing, the next best thing is the wrong thing, and the worst thing you can do is nothing."

— Theodore Roosevelt

If there's one word that captures the essence of what is occurring in the world today, it's "change." Downsizing, reorganizing, and cutting costs, are now the norm for survival. No industry is exempt; there are no sacred cows. Even the most venerable and conservative institutions are undergoing significant change just to survive. For this industry, in spite of the improvement that many equipment distributors are reporting, a full recovery is not predicted to occur in the immediate future.

There are challenges in change. Although change is occurring all around us, no one likes to have change imposed on themselves without being involved. There is a sense of comfort in having a routine and the knowledge knowing where things are, whom to contact for information and an expectation of what to expect. Change can disrupt that routine and can often shake our confidence, increase stress levels, and decrease productivity.

Transformational change must be more than just a change in software, hardware, and process improvements. People must be part of the equation, but not just adapting to the changes around them. Like technology and business process that enhance performance, the knowledge, skills, abilities, and behaviors of the individual employees have an equal investment in driving operational performance.

Following are ten effective tips for successfully implementing change in your organization.

1. Communicate the reason for the change along with the change vision. Change is driven and communicated from the top down. Each level of management must understand, support, and align to the proposed change.

2. Involve the leadership team in strategic planning and develop them to be change champions.

    The entire leadership team needs to be involved with creating your organization's operational strategy and on board with the changes the team has decided to implement. Remind them to think and act as dynamic leaders who will provide the inspiration and encouragement to your entire workforce.

3. Establish a culture of open communication. Communication is a two-way street. Too often managers disseminate information in the form of an email and expect that everyone will read, understand, and act on the message. Create a communication plan where messages are targeted and where the exchange of information goes two ways.

4. Establish a "change" team

Appoint people who have truly shown leadership abilities to lead the way to deploy the change management process. These individuals should have high levels of credibility among their peers, who have a strong knowledge of the business, can think outside of the box, and has a good understanding of the problems faced by the organization.

5. Allow change to be internalized

Large-scale change is a learning event and will need time to internalize. The commitment curve illustrates how change is adopted across the seven stages: Contact - Disseminates the preliminary information; Awareness - Broadens the knowledge of the change; Understanding - Draws relationships between individuals and the change; Positive Perception - Building understanding of the perceived benefits; Adoption - Builds the organizational structures; Institutionalization - Measures and aligns the organization; and Internalization - Develops new behaviors to support the core values.

6. Be in tune to difficulties some may be experiencing

Recognize that change affects each individual differently. Some people are more adaptable than others. Many top performers will roll up their sleeves to make things work – moving out of their comfort zone instantly. Others may be completely overwhelmed. Let them know you understand the challenges they are facing and that you are there to help them through it. Here, remember the importance of open communication. Keep your door open to allow people to come in to discuss any apprehension. Provide a comfortable environment where people can air their concerns.

7. Manage resistance

    Human beings are creatures of habit. They like doing things the same way. Doing things differently takes them out of their comfort zone. Some people may resist and hold back their team and, consequently, your company. Talk to any person who comes to work with a chip on his or her shoulder. Ask the person who is making negative remarks and pulling down morale to refrain from doing so. Explain that everyone is working hard pull together and deliver their best performance each day. Ask them what you can do to help them.

8. Be a role model, lead by example

    It is up to you as their leader to maintain employee morale through change. Set the tone; be a role model and be an example for others to follow. During tough times, people will always watch how their leader is acting. Don't let your guard down when it comes to your attitude. When the economy is down, you have to be up.

9. Take the time to instruct and coach

    To reduce the loss of productivity during the change, make sure your people have the necessary skills to succeed. Instruction must be a top priority. The time and money you invest in training and coaching will eventually pay off in increased profits and service quality. As you look at the changes you plan to implement, ask yourself these training-related questions: What is the level of competence needed to support the changes in our company and help us make it through these challenging times? What training will be needed to bring the staff up to that level of competence? What training is needed on new products, procedures, and especially product support? It is the area where you are likely to make the most profit in the environment.

10. Alleviate job stress

Meeting the demands placed upon people during the change process requires managing the increased job stress for yourself and others. During the change initiative, productivity is on a decline since key people are tasked to perform the change work often in addition to performing their regularly assigned tasks. Other employees not assigned to the project have to work harder to take up the slack. These people may often feel left out and less important. These feelings create job strain and stress. After the change gets implemented, the new systems and processes can be confusing and add to the stress level. One way to alleviate job stress is to recognize the work efforts of those involved and celebrate success.

The overall objective:

Managing change is critical to the success of any initiative. No matter how high-tech the new systems may offer, or how well defined the business processes may be, these will result in little value if they are not accepted and supported by the individual employees.

ABOUT THE AUTHOR

With nearly 30 years of consulting experience, Dr. George B. Lampere has been studying organizational culture and assisting senior leaders to develop adaptive and constructive behaviors that will not only support, but will sustain an environment of continuous change to improve operational performance. His work gets very exciting especially when it is related to large-scale transformational change, this is when his work pays off for his clients. Dr. Lampere guides the organization through his structured transformation approach which he calls the Integrated Performance Solution, or IPS. He refers to the approach as a solution because the IPS aids in solving a complex transformational problem based upon defined and measurable outcomes.

His experience spans a wide variety of industries within the public and private sectors. His success regardless of the industry or sector is understanding the behaviors that exist within these organizations and the barriers that control them. Whether it is an issue of operational performance, quality, safety or security, understanding the organizational cultural differences between departments and physical locations and the drivers that promote those behaviors is the key to making change that is lasting.

OTHER PUBLICATIONS:

Dr. Lampere's first book, Business Cards: Transforming the Organization One Card at a time, published by Greer-Joel Publishing (September 1, 2012) ISBN-13: 978-0615643878 describes the activities and sequencing needed for a successful transformational change. The book is based on a matrix that identifies four drivers of operational performance: People and Organizational Systems; Business Processes; Technology; and Information and Knowledge Management. Activities are divided into four groups: Strategic, Tactical, Operational, and Functional. The activities must be sequenced and aligned across each driver before proceeding to the next level. Skipping an activity or performing it out of sequence increases the risk of failure.

Dr. Lampere is the founder and CEO of Navitsumo Consulting Ltd. Additional support materials can be found on his website: www.glampere. com, and on Slideshare.net.

Learn more about the author

For additional information contact
(847) 794-8910
E-Mail: glampere@glampere.com
www.glampere.com

www.ingramcontent.com/pod-product-compliance
Lightning Source LLC
Chambersburg PA
CBHW060340200326
41519CB00011BA/1995